REVISED CHARTER

OF THE

CITY OF KENOSHA,

1866.

THE

REVISED CHARTER

AND

ORDINANCES

OF THE

CITY OF KENOSHA,

WITH THE

BY-LAWS OF THE COUNCIL.

Kenosha:

PRINTED AT THE TELEGRAPH BOOK AND JOB OFFICE.

1866.

REVISED CHARTER.

CHAPTER I.

CITY AND WARD BOUNDARIES.

SECTION 1. *The people of the State of Wisconsin, represented in senate and assembly, do enact as follows:* The district of country in the county of Kenosha and state of Wisconsin, known and described as follows, to wit: The south-east quarter of section thirty; fractional section thirty-two; the east half of section thirty-one; the south-east quarter of the north-west quarter and the east half of the south-west quarter section thirty-one, in town two; the north-east quarter, and the north-east quarter of the north-west quarter of section six, and the north half of fractional section five, in town one, all in range twenty-three east, together with that part of Lake Michigan due east of the same within one fourth of a mile thereof, shall be a city by the name of Kenosha. Boundaries.

SEC. 2. The inhabitants of said city shall be a corporation by the name of the "City of Kenosha," and by that name may sue and be sued, complain and defend in any court, contract and be contracted with, make and use a common seal, and alter it at pleasure, and take, hold and purchase, lease and convey such real and personal estate as the purposes General powers.

of the corporation may require within or without the limits of said city; and shall otherwise possess the general powers of municipal corporations at common law.

Ward boundaries. [Amended.] SEC. 3. The city of Kenosha shall be divided into three wards, as follows: All that part of said city described as follows: Commencing on the lake shore on the south line of Wisconsin street, thence west on said line to the east line of West Main street, thence to the south-east corner of Durkee's western addition, thence west along the south line of said addition and the south line of block five of Fisk's first addition to the west line of said block five, thence west to the west line of said city, thence north to the south line of Grand street extended, thence east on the south line of said street to the centre of the creek, thence along the centre of the creek to the mouth of the harbor, thence east to the east line of the city, thence south to a point due east of the place of beginning, thence west to the place of beginning shall constitute the first ward of the city.

That part of said city lying north of the first ward shall constitute the second ward of the city.

That part of said city lying south of the first ward shall constitute the third ward of the city.

CHAPTER II.

CITY OFFICERS.

Municipality. [Amended.] SECTION 1. The municipal government of the city shall consist of a common council, composed of a mayor and three aldermen from each ward.

SEC. 2. A mayor, a treasurer, a clerk, a railroad commissioner, a superintendent of schools, an assessor, a marshal, and one justice of the peace for the city at large, and one alderman, one school commissioner, and one constable for each ward shall be elected annually by the people. Elective offices. [Amended.]

SEC. 3. A city attorney, harbor master, poor master, city physician, chief engineer of the fire department, surveyor, a chief of police, and one or more street supervisors, and fire wardens, inspectors, sextons, and all such other officers as may be deemed necessary for the proper mannagement of the affairs of said city, may be appointed by the common council, which officers shall hold their offices severally during the pleasure of the council, and at such compensation as the council shall prescribe. Appointees, &c., their compensation.

SEC. 4. None but electors of said city shall be eligible to or qualified to hold an elective office created by this act. Who eligible.

SEC. 5. The mayor, treasurer, clerk, railroad commissioner, superintendent of schools, assessor, and marshal shall hold their offices respectively for the term of one year, and until their successors are elected and qualified. The aldermen and school commissioners shall hold their offices respectively for the term of two years, and until their successors shall be elected and qualified; *provided*, That officers elected to fill vacancies, shall respectively hold for the unexpired term only, or until their successors shall be elected and qualified. Term of office.

SEC. 6. The aldermen, school commissioners, and the justice of the peace, elected at the next annual election, shall be successors to the present aldermen, school commissioners, and justice of the peace respectively, whose terms of office expire at that time. The aldermen, school commissioners and justice of the peace, elected one year thereafter respectively, shall be successors to those aldermen and school commissioners, and of that justice of the peace, whose terms of office expire one year after the next election.

Elective office, when vacant.

SEC. 7. If any officer elected exclusively by any ward, shall remove from such ward, or if any officer of such city shall die, resign, refuse to act, or remove from the city, his office shall thereby become vacant.

Vacancy, how filled.

SEC. 8. Whenever any vacancy shall occur of any elective office, such vacancy shall be filled by special election.

County supervisors, how chosen [Amended]

SEC. 9. There shall be chosen by the electors of each ward, at the annual election of said city, one supervisor for each ward, to represent such ward in the county board of supervisors, and said supervisors so chosen, are hereby empowered to sit in the county board of supervisors, with the same rights and powers, as are, or may be by law prescribed for, and exercised by other members of said board.

CHAPTER III.

OF ELECTIONS.

Municipal election, when and how held.

SECTION 1. An election shall be held in the several wards of said city on the first Tuesday in April in each year at such place in each ward, as shall be designated by the council, for the choice of the city and ward officers, authorized by this act to be elected annually by the people, and of the time and place of such election, ten days' previous public notice shall be given in such manner as the common council may determine.

Special elections, when and how held.

SEC. 2. Special elections for the purpose provided for in this act, may be held on any day, and on the hours of any day designated by the common council; but otherwise shall be conducted, and the result thereof canvassed, certified and returned in all respects, as near as practicable, in like manner as the annual election for city and ward officers; except that returns for special elections need not be made to the clerk of the board of supervisors.

Plurality to elect.

SEC. 3. At any city election in said city, a plurality of all the votes cast in the city for any person for any city office; and a plurality of all the votes cast in any ward for any person for any office of such ward, shall constitute an election.

Proceedings on tie.

SEC. 4. Where two or more persons shall receive an equal number of votes for the same office; the election as to such office shall be determined by the casting of lots in the presence of the common council, at such time and in such manner as it shall direct.

Qualifications of voters.

SEC. 5. Every qualified elector for members of the legislature of this state, who may reside within the ward where he may offer his vote, shall be deemed a qualified voter of said city, and shall be entitled to vote in the ward in which he resides for any officer in the city required by this act to be elected; *provided*, That no elector shall be deemed a resident of any ward, unless he shall have lodged in such ward for twenty days next preceeding such election.

Inspectors and clerks.

SEC. 6. All elections in said city, shall be held and conducted by the aldermen of each ward who shall be the inspectors of elections and shall take the usual oaths or affirmations as prescribed by the general laws of the state, to be taken by the judges and inspectors of elections, and they shall have the power to appoint clerks of such elections, and to administer to them the necessary oaths.

Mode of election.

SEC. 7. The manner of conducting elections, held under this act, and of contesting the same, the keeping of the poll lists, except as otherwise provided in this act, shall be the same, as nearly as practicable, as now provided by law for general state elections.

Oath on challenge.

SEC. 8. If any person offering to vote at any city election shall be challenged by any elector of the ward in which such vote is offered, before receiving the vote of such person, one of the inspectors shall require him to take the following oath: You do solemnly swear (or affirm) that you are twenty-one years of age, that you are a citizen of the United States (or have declared your intentions to become such, conformable to the laws of the United States on the subject of naturalization,) that you have resided in this state one year, that you are now a resident of this ward, and have lodged therein for twenty days next preceeding this election, and that you have not voted at this election, and that you have made no bet or wager, depending upon the result of this election. And if the person offering to vote, shall take such oath, his vote shall be received.

Penalty for illegal voting.

SEC. 9. Any person who shall illegally vote at any election held under this act shall be punished according to the laws of this state for illegal voting.

Returns, how made.

SEC. 10. After the closing of the polls, the ballots shall be counted in the manner provided by law, and the returns shall be returned sealed to the city clerk, within three days after the election, and thereupon the common council shall meet and canvass the same and declare the result of the election.

Informalities, how corrected.

SEC. 11. If any election provided for in this act shall for any cause not be held at the time prescribed it shall not be considered a sufficient reason for arresting, suspending, or dissolving the said corporation, but such election may be held at any time thereafter, by order of the common council, of which time ten days' public notice shall be given; and further, if any of the duties enjoined by this act, at a time herein specified, or specified by any ordinance of said city, are not then done, the city council may appoint another time upon which the said duties may be performed.

CHAPTER IV.

OFFICERS, THEIR POWERS AND DUTIES.

Who to take oath.

SECTION 1. Every person elected or appointed to any office under this act, shall, before he enters upon the duties of his office, take and subscribe the oath of office and file the same, duly certified, with the city clerk.

Who to execute bonds

SEC. 2. The treasurer, clerk, marshal, railroad commissioner, constable, and such other officers as the council may direct, shall severally, before they enter upon the duties of their respective offices, execute to the city of Kenosha a bond, with at least two sureties, to be approved by the common council, and said bond shall contain such penal sum, and such conditions as the council may deem proper; and the council may from time to time require new or additional bonds, and remove from office any officer refusing or neglecting to give the same.

Election of president of council.

SEC. 3. The members of the city council shall on the first Monday after each annual election, or so soon thereafter as may be practicable, elect from their own body, a president to preside in their meetings in the absence of the mayor.

When to serve.

SEC. 4. In case of the vacancy of the office of mayor, or of his being unable to perform the duties of his office, by reason of absence, sickness or any other cause, the president of the city council shall be vested with all the powers and perform all the duties of mayor, until the mayor shall resume his office, or the vacancy shall be filled by a new election.

President pro tem. when to serve.

SEC. 5. In case of absence or inability of both the mayor and the president of the city council, a president pro tem. shall be elected, and for the time being shall discharge the duties of mayor.

Duties of mayor.

SEC. 6. The mayor shall preside at all meetings of the city council when present; he shall be the chief executive officer and head of the police of the city. It shall be his duty to recommend in writing to the city council such measures as he may deem expedient; he shall sign all commissions, licences, and permits, which may be granted by the city council; he shall maintain peace and good order, and see that the laws of the state and ordinances of the city are observed and executed; shall be entitled to vote on all questions before the council when present, and shall administer oaths or affirmations, and to take and certify acknowledgements of deeds and other instruments in writing; as a judicial officer, he shall have all the power, and exercise the jurisdiction of justices of the peace, in this state, by giving the bonds required by law; and in case of riot or other public disturbances, he may appoint as many special or temporary constables as he may deem proper.

When may vote.

May appoint constables.

Duties of treasurer.

Sec. 7. The treasurer shall receive all moneys belonging to the city and keep an accurate and detailed account of all receipts and expenditures in such manner as the council shall direct. He shall pay no money from the treasury, except upon the order of the council, signed by the mayor and countersigned by the clerk, which order shall specify the amount of money to be drawn and the object of the appropriation; and such orders shall not bear interest except by special vote of the city council. He shall as often as once in three months, and as much oftener as the council may require, return all such orders paid by him, with a list thereof, which list shall specify the sums paid upon each order, and the purpose for which appropriated. He shall report to the common council once in three months, and oftener if required, a statement of the condition of the treasury and the several funds thereof; one of which statements shall be made within fifteen days of every annual election.

To report quarterly.

SEC. 8 The clerk shall keep the corporate seal, and all papers and records of the city. He shall attend all meetings of the council, and keep a record of its proceedings. He shall draw and countersign all orders on the treasury, or for sums duly appropriated by the council, and shall keep the stubs of such orders; he shall further keep full and accurate accounts of all sums so appropriated. which accounts shall specify the purpose of such appropriations, in books provided for that purpose; he shall record all orders and ordinances adopted by the council, in a book kept exclusively for that purpose, and perform such other duties pertaining to his office as are prescribed for town clerks by the general laws of the state, or the common council may direct; he shall

Duties of clerk

To record ordinances.

have power to administer oaths, and affirmations; and copies of all papers filed in his office, and transcripts from any of the records thereof, certified to by him under the corporate seal, shall be evidence in all courts, in the like manner as if the originals were produced. May administer oaths.

SEC. 9. The Marshal shall perform such duties as shall be prescribed by the common council for the preservation of the public peace, and for the collection of license moneys and fines; he shall possess the powers of constable by the laws of this state, and shall receive like fees. Duties of marshal. To have powers of constable.

SEC. 10. The mayor, or acting mayor, each and every alderman, marshal, each and every justice of the peace, and constable of the city of Kenosha, or any other person or persons appointed by the council for such purpose, shall be officers of the peace, and suppress, in a summary manner, all rioting and disorderly behavior, in a manner consistent with the ordinances of said city, within the limits thereof, and for such purpose may command the assistance of all bystanders, and if need be, of all citizens and military companies, and if any person, bystander, military officer, or private of such company shall refuse to aid in maintaining the peace when so required, every such person shall forfeit and pay such fine as may be prescribed by ordinance of the city council in such case provided; and in all cases where the civil power may be required to suppress riotous or or disorderly behavior, the superior or senior officer Who peace officers.

in the order mentioned in this section, shall direct the proceedings.

Duties and powers of officers; who to prescribe.

SEC. 11. The common council shall have power to require further and other duties of all officers, whose duties are herein prescribed, and to prescribe the powers and duties of all officers appointed or elected to any office under this act, whose duties are not herein specifically mentioned, to fix the compensation of all such officers, and to impose penalties for non-performance or neglect in the discharge of any duties imposed by the ordinances or by this act.

Aldermen not to contract.

SEC. 12. No alderman shall be a party to, or interested in any contract with the city, without the expressed unanimous consent of the council.

Justices of peace; when to pay over fines.

SEC. 13. The justices of the peace of said city shall, as often as once in six months, report to the common council a list of all proceedings instituted before them on behalf of the city, or under its ordinances, with the disposition thereof; and shall at the same time account for and pay over the amount of all penalties and costs collected by them as the result of such proceedings.

Compensation of mayor and aldermen. [Amended.]

SEC. 14 The compensation of the mayor or any alderman, shall not exceed one dollar and fifty cents for each session of the council, unless for specific services otherwise performed, and in such case compensation shall not exceed two dollars per day.

Penalty for non-delivery of effects by city officers.

SEC. 15. If any person having been an officer of said city shall not, within ten days after notification and request, deliver to his successor in office, all the property, papers and effects of every description, in his possession, belonging to said city, or appertaining to the office he held, he shall forfeit and pay for the use of the city one hundred dollars, besides all damages caused by his neglect or refusal so to deliver; said penalty to be recovered before any court of competent jurisdiction, in the same manner as penalties for the violation of city ordinances are collected.

CHAPTER V.

THE COMMON COUNCIL.

SECTION 1. A majority of the members of the common council shall constitute a quorum, who shall have power to compel the attendance of absent members. Quorum, how constituted.

SEC. 2. The council shall hold meetings, at such times and place as it may appoint. The mayor may call special meetings by notice to each of the aldermen. Meetings, when held.

SEC. 3. The council shall determine the rules of its own proceedings, and be the judge of the election and qualification of its own members. Prerogative of council.

SEC. 4. The style of all ordinances adopted by the council, shall be: Be it ordained by the common council of the city of Kenosha. Enacting phrase.

SEC. 5. The common council shall have the management and control of the finances, and of all the property, real personal and mixed, belonging to the Finances and property; who to control, &c.

corporation; shall settle all claims and demands against the city, settle with the treasurer annually, and make out and publish accounts of the receipts and expenditures of the city annually, for the information of the citizens.

Orders &c., to be published.

SEC. 6. Any law, ordinance, order, regulation and by-law, imposing any fine, penalty or forfeiture, shall be passed by an affirmative vote of a majority of the common council, signed by the mayor, and published in one or more newspapers of the city before the same shall be in force; and all such laws, ordinances, orders, regulations and by-laws so published, shall be recorded immediately after such publication, together with an affidavit of such publication, which affidavit shall be made by the printer, publisher or office-foreman of the newspaper in which the publication was made; and such affidavit so recorded shall at all times be deemed sufficient evidence of such publication.

Council may alter rules, &c., at discretion.

SEC. 7. The common council shall have full power and authority to make, enact, ordain, establish, publish, enforce, alter, modify, amend and repeal all such ordinances, rules and by-laws for the government and good order of the city, for the protection of property for the suppression of vice, for the prevention and punishment of crime, for the benefit of the commerce, trade and health of the city as they shall deem expedient. It shall also have power to declare and impose penalties, and to enforce the same by fine or imprisonment, or in any other manner they may provide, against any person or persons who may violate any of the provisions of such ordinance, rule or by-laws as are hereby declared to be and to have the force of law.

Specific powers.

SEC, 8. Beside other powers in this act granted to the common council of the city of Kenosha, said council shall have the power by ordinance, order or resolution.

May license shows and liquor venders.

1st. To license and to regulate auctions, the exhibitions of common showmen or shows of any kind or the exhibition of any natural or artificial curiosities, caravans, circuses, concerts or theatrical performances; and to restrain and prohibit any person from vending or dealing in spirituons, fermented or vinous liquors, unless duly licensed by the common council.

May prohibit gaming.

2nd. To restrain and prohibit all descriptions of gaming and fraudulent devices and practices, and all playing of cards, dice, or other games of chance for the purpose of gaming in said city.

May suppress and restrain disorderly houses.

3d. To prevent any riots, noise, disturbance or disorderly assemblage, suppress and restrain disorderly houses or groceries, houses of ill-fame, billiard tables, nine or ten pin alleys or tables, shows and exhibitions, to authorize the destruction of all instruments or devices used for the purpose of gaming, and to abate nuisances.

May abate nuisances.

4th. To compel the owner or occupant of any grocery, cellar, tallow-chandler's shop, soap factory, tannery, stable, barn, privy, sewer, or other unwholesome or nauseous houses or places, to cleanse, remove or abate the same from time to time, as often as it may be deemed necessary for the health, comfort and convenience of the inhabitants of the city.

May regulate markets and keeping of gunpowder.

5th. To direct the location and management of all slaughter houses and markets, to establish rules for and license venders of gunpowder, and regulate the storage and keeping and conveying of gunpowder or other combustible materials.

May remove encumbrances

6th. To prevent the encumbering of the streets, sidewalks, lanes, alleys, or public grounds with carriages, carts, wagons, sleighs, sleds, boxes, lumber, fire-wood, or other materials or substance whatever.

May prevent improper driving and bathing

7th. To prevent horse racing, immoderate driving or riding in the streets, and to regulate the places of bathing and swimming in the waters within the limits of said city.

May restrain animals.

8th. To restrain the running at large of cattle, swine, sheep, horses. poultry and geese, and to authorize the distraining and sale of the same.

May regulate keeping of dogs.

9th. To prevent the running at large of dogs, and to authorize their destruction in a summary manner when at large, contrary to the ordinance, or to impose a tax on the same.

May prevent deposit of putrid substances.

10th. To prevent any person from bringing, depositing, or having within said city any putrid carcass, or any unwholsome substance, and to require the removal of the same by any person who shall have upon his premises any such substance, or any putrid or unsound beef, pork, fish, hides or skins of any kind; and in default, to authorize the removal by some competent officer, at the expense of such person or persons.

11th. To make and establish public pounds, pumps, wells, cisterns and reservoirs, and to provide for the erection of water-works for the supply of watea to the inhabitants of said city, or any ward therein, to erect lamps, and regulate and license hacks, cabs, drays, carts and the charges of hackmen, cabmen and draymen, within the limits of said city. May establish water works, and license hacks, &c.,

12th. To establish and regulate boards of health provide hospitals, poor houses, and cemetery grounds and regulate the burial of the dead. May provide poor houses, hospitals, &c.

13th. To regulate the building of bridges, and provide for the security and protection of the same. May regulate the building of bridges.

14th. To prevent all persons riding or driving any horse, ox, mule, cattle or other animal on the side-walks in said city, or in any way damage to such side-walks. May prevent misuse of side-walks.

15th. To prevent the shooting of fire-arms or crackers, except by special permission of the common council, and to prevent the exhibition of any fire-works in every situation which may be considered by the common council dangerous to the city, or any property therein, or annoying to any citizen thereof. May prevent fire-works and use of fire arms.

16th. To restrain drunkards, immoderate drinking, or obscenity in the streets or public places, and provide for arresting, removing and punishing any person or persons who may be guilty of the same. May restrain drunkards.

May appoint policemen.

17th. To appoint policemen, watchmen and firemen, prescribe their duties and punish their delinquencies.

May regulate markets

18th. To establish public markets, and make rules and regulations for the government of the same; to appoint suitable officers for overseeing and regulating such markets, and to restrain all persons from interrupting or interfering with the due observance of such rules and regulations.

May appoint inspectors.

19th. To regulate the place and manner of weighing and selling hay, of measuring and selling fuel, fish, lime, and other articles, and appoint suitable persons to superintend, conduct, or inspect the same.

May remove nuisances.

20th. To compel the owner or occupant of any building or ground to remove the snow, dirt, or rubbish from the sidewalk, street or alley opposite thereto, and to compel such owner or occupant to remove from the lot owned or occupied by him, all such substances as the city shall direct, and in his default to authorize the removal or destruction thereof by some suitable officer, at the expense of such owner or occupant.

May authorize issue of licenses.

21st. To authorize the mayor, or other proper officer of the city, to grant and issue licenses, and direct the manner of issuing and registering thereof, and the fees to be paid therefor.

May regulate use of locomotives

22d. To regulate the use of locomotive engines, and to direct and control the location of railroad tracks and depot grounds within the city.

23d. To direct and regulate the planting and preserving of ornamental trees in the streets and public grounds. May direct planting of trees.

24th. To establish harbor and dock limits, and regulate the locality and manner of construction of and wharves docks, along the banks of Pike creek, within the limits of said city. May establish dock limits.

25. To lease the wharfing privileges of Pike creek, within the limits of said city, at the ends of streets, upon such terms and conditions as may be usual in the leasing of other real estate, reserving such rents as may be agreed upon, and employing such remedies in case of non-performance of any covenants in any such lease as are given by law in other cases. May lease wharves.

26th. To erect or purchase such public buildings as may be necessary for public use, and to build regulate and lease dredges, scows, wharves, docks, or piers on the harbor, or at the ends of streets or alleys. May purchase buildings, scows, &c.

27th. To prevent and remove all obstructions within, or encroachments upon the harbor, and otherwise improve and protect it by dredging, piering widening, deepening or straightening the same, as may be deemed necessary for the public good. May regulate use of harbor, &c.

28th. To use the jail of Kenosha county for the imprisonment of offenders against the ordinances, rules, or by-laws, and persons so imprisoned shall be in the custody of the sheriff of the county, and their expenses shall be paid in the same manner as the May use Kenosha county jail.

expenses of persons imprisoned under the general laws of the state.

City plat to be evidence &c.

SEC. 9. The common council shall, within six months from the passage of this act, cause an accurate plat of said city to be made, which plat shall contain and specify the boundaries of all streets, alleys, public grounds, and of all lots, blocks, and out-lots, with their numbers, and other lands in said city; and said plat when approved by the council and certified by the mayor and clerk, shall be recorded, and be legal evidence of all the boundaries and numbers therein, in all courts and places.

CHAHTER VI.

OF TAXATION.

General power of taxation.

SECTION 1. For the purpose of meeting any expenditure authorized by the common council under the provisions of this act, or ordinance of said city, or to defray the current expenses of said city, the common council shall have power to levy and collect annually a tax on all such real and personal property, or capital of any kind within said city, subject to taxation by the laws for levying the taxes of this state for the time being, and the money so raised shall constitute the general fund.

Annual tax to be levied

SEC. 2. The common council shall annually levy and collect a school tax on all the real and personal estate, to meet the expenses of purchasing grounds for school purposes, for building and repairing school houses, and for the support and maintenance of schools.

When tax may be more frequently levied.

Sec. 3. The common council shall have power annually, or more frequently, to levy and collect a tax on all the lots and land in said city, not including any improvements thereon, to pay the bonded debt of the city or the interest thereon, and shall have power to issue new bonds when necessary to meet such indebtedness, for such time and at such rates of interest as they may deem expedient; but bonds shall be issued for no other purpose than to meet such indebtedness, except as hereinafter provided.

May borrow money by ordinance.

Sec. 4. For any purpose aside from what is otherwise specifically provided for in this chapter, the common council shall have power to levy and collect special taxes, in the same manner that other taxes are levied and collected, and such special taxes may be levied upon such real and personal estate in the city as the council may determine; or the common council may borrow on the corporate credit of the city any sum of money for any term of time, at any rate of interest, and payable at any place deemed expedient, issuing bonds or scrip therefor; *Provided*, That no such tax shall be levied or money borrowed except as shall be provided by ordinance, which ordinance shall in each case specify the amount of such tax or loan and all other essential particulars relating thereto, and be approved by a majority of the voters of the city possessed of a freehold estate, or occupy-

Ordinance to be voted on.

ing lots upon which they pay the taxes, voting at a special election which may be called for that purpose.

Poll tax.

Sec. 5. There shall be two days' work performed annually on highways, streets and alleys by each male person who by the laws of the state is subject to perform highway work, such person to perform such labor within the ward where he resides, under the direction of the aldermen of the ward, or such street commissioners or supervisors as the common council may appoint, but any such person may at his option pay at a ratio of seventy-five cents per day, for every day he may be so bound to labor, and in default of the payment of such money, or the performance of such labor, any street commissioner or supervisor may sue for and collect such money by an action of debt in the name of the city of Kenosha, with fifty per cent. damages on the same, together with cost of suit, before the mayor of the city or any justice of the peace; and in all such cases the process shall be by warrant, and no stay of execution upon any judgment rendered on such suit shall be taken or allowed.

Supervisors may sue for and collect.

Exempt property.

Sec. 6. The property exempt from taxation by the laws of the state or of the United States shall not be subject to taxation for the support of the city government, or for the payment of its debts and liabilities.

Of collection.

Sec. 7. The council shall by ordinance prescribe the time in which highway taxes may be levied and collected, and returns thereof be made by the street commissioners, or supervisors.

CHAPTER VII.

OF HIGHWAYS AND PUBLIC GROUNDS.

SECTION 1. The common council shall have power to lay out public grounds, streets, and alleys, and to alter, widen, contract, straighten, and vacate the same; and all streets and alleys laid out by the council shall be highways.

May regulate streets, &c. and alter or lay out the same.

SEC. 2. Within twenty days after the presentation to the council of any petition of any persons interested to lay out highways or public grounds, the common council may choose by ballot five disinterested freeholders residing in said city as commissioners to ascertain and determine: 1st. The necessity of taking any private property for laying out such highway or public ground petitioned for. 2d. The damages and recompense due the owners respectively of any such private property necessary to be taken. 3d. What persons will be benefited by such improvement, and to assess the damages and expenses of such improvement on the real estate of persons so benefitted in proportion as nearly as may be to the benefits resulting to each.

May appoint commissioners.

Damages, how assessed.

Sec. 3. The said commissioners, not less than ten days before they shall proceed to the discharge of their duties, as provided in the preceding section, shall cause notice to be given to all persons interested or to the agents of such persons, either personally or by written information left at the residence of any

Notice, how given.

such person, of the time when and the place where they will meet for the purpose of determining the necessity of taking any private property for the public use, and of awarding damages therefor, as aforesaid; or in case any such interested persons shall be unknown or non-resident, and have no agent in the city, notice of such meeting may be given to all such persons by publication in one of the newspapers of the city, for such time as the commissioners may deem sufficient.

Commissioners to take oath.

Sec. 4. The commissioners aforesaid shall be sworn faithfully to execute their duties according to the best of their ability; they shall view the premises, and if necessary, may adminster oaths to witnesses, receive any legal evidence, and may adjourn from day to day.

Return of commissioners, how made.

Sec. 5. Within twenty days after their appointment, said commissioners shall make return to the council, under their hands, of the amount of benefits, damages and expenses assessed by them, with a description of the property assessed, and the proportion of such assessment for each lot.

City clerk to give notice.

Sec. 6. When such return has been made, as provided in the preceding section, the city clerk shall cause notice to be given to all interested persons, or the agents of such persons, of the award of the commissioners, which notice shall either be personal or by written information left at the residence of any such interested person, except in case of unknown or non-resident persons, without agents residing in the city, so interested, in which case such notice shall be given by publication for one or more weeks, in some newspaper published in the city; and such notice shall state that on or after a day specified therein, (said day to be fixed by the common council, and to be not less than two days from date of such notice,) the award of the commissioners will be confirmed by the council, unless objections to the same are made to the common council in writing, by some person interested, previous to or on such day specified.

Whenaward to be given.

SEC. 7. If no objections are made, as provided in the preceeding section, the confirmation of the award of the commissioners, the consent of any party or parties interested shall be deemed given; and any further or other proceedings on the part of any party or parties interested shall be deemed waived; and the council shall proceed to confirm such award by a final order, and when such award is so confirmed, the assessment made therein shall be a lien on the property assessed, and be collected and made payable in the same manner as annual taxes are collected and made payable.

When consent to be given.

Assessment when to be a lien.

SEC. 8. The council shall have power at any time during the proceedings herein provided for, to remove any commissioner, and to appoint others in place of such as may be removed, refuse, neglect, or be unable from any cause to serve.

Commissioners, how removed.

SEC. 9. The land required to be taken for laying out any public ground, street, or alley shall not be appropriated for such purpose until the damages

Damages, how tendered.

awarded thereof, shall be paid or tendered to such owner or his agent; or when such owner or agent cannot conveniently found, be deposited with the treasurer for the benefit of such owner.

Equitable compensation.

SEC. 10. If the lands necessary in any case to be taken as hereinbefore provided belong to different persons, or be subject to lease or contract for conveyance thereof duly reccorded, the injury done to any person in any manner so interested, respectively, may be awarded by the commissioners, less the benefits resulting to them respectively from the proposed improvement.

Appeal, how taken.

SEC. 11. Whenever any final order has been made for taking any private property for public use, as hereinbefore provided, without the consent of the ower thereof, as hereinbefore provided; or whenever any person shall claim greater damages than shall be awarded by the commissioners for property so taken, and shall not waive his right to further and other proceedings, as hereinbefor provided, such owner or owners may appeal from any final order of the council for opening or widening any street, alley, or public ground to the circuit court of Kenosha county, by filing notice of such appeal with the city clerk, at any time within two weeks after the passage of such final order by the council.

Duty of clerk of court.

SEC. 12. Whenever notice of such appeal shall be filed with the city clerk, as provided in the preceeding section, the clerk shall within ten days thereafter return to the clerk of the circuit court of Kenosha county the name of the party filing such notice, together with the award of the commissioners, and the order of the council relating thereto, and on the trial of such suit the city shall be plaintiff and the appellant shall be the defendant, and otherwise said suit shall be subject to the same rules and regulations as other appealed cases.

Jury to find the land was necessarily taken, &c. Sum of damages.

On the trial of such appeal, the jury shall find as well the necessity of taking such land for the uses aforesaid as the amount of compensation paid to said appellant for taking the same, and the court upon verdict rendered therein, shall have power to confirm or annul the order of the common council appealed from, according to the verdict of the jury, and may give judgment, vesting in the city for the uses aforesaid, the property described in the award of the commissioners as belonging to the appellant, upon the payment by the city of the amount of damages found by the jury; and in case the appellant shall recover the same amount of damages by said suit as was awarded him by the commissioners aforesaid, or a less amount than was so awarded, he shall be adjudged to to pay the costs of suit; in all other cases the city shall pay the costs of suit.

Who to pay costs.

Survey to be recorded.

SEC. 13. Whenever any public ground, street, or alley shall be laid out, widened, contracted, straightened, vacated or otherwise altered according to the provisions of this chapter, the common council shall cause an accurate survey and profile of every such alteration to be filed with the city clerk and recorded.

CHAPTER VIII.

OF STREET IMPROVEMENTS.

Of highways.

SECTION 1. The common council shall have power to cause any highway to be graded, levelled gravelled, or paved, and to keep the same in repair.

Sidewalks, sewers, &c.

SEC. 2. The common council shall have power to cause cross and side-walks, main drains, and sewers, and private drains, to be constructed and laid, re-laid, removed, cleansed or repaired, and to regulate the same.

Petitions for improvement, when may be granted.

SEC. 3. When a majority of all the owners of real estate bounding both sides of any street or part of a street shall petition the common council to order such street or part of street graded, levelled, gravelled, or paved, or to construct a sewer therein; or whenever the majority of all the owners of real esteate bounding one side of any highway, shall petition the common co ıncil to cause side-walks to be laid on the side of such highway, bounded by such real estate, such petition may be granted and an order be made in accordance therewith, which order will specify as nearly as may be, ths locality and manner of the improvement proposed, and notice shall be given to all persons interested, personally or by publishing such order one week in some paper published in the city.

SEC. 4. Whenever any order shall have been made for grading, levelling, gravelling, or paving any highway; or for building any side-walk as herein provided, the street supervisor of the ward in which such work is ordered to be done, or such other person as the council may designate as street supervisor for that special purpose, shall immediately after the publication of this order, cause to be performed such work in manner specified in such order, and under the direction of the aldermen of the ward in which such work is to be done, and when such work is completed, such supervisor or other person shall immediately thereafter return to the city clerk an account in detail of the expense thereof.

Notice, how given.

Work, how may be done

Returns how made.

SEC. 5. The aggregate expense of any improvement provided for in any such order of the common council as hereinbefore provided in this chapter, shall be assessed by the common council on the lots lying upon or bounding the highway upon which such improvement is made, according to the relative benefit accruing to each lot; and a tax shall be levied therefor upon said lots, and such tax shall become a lien upon the lots so levied upon, and shall be collected in like manner, as other taxes levied under this act.

Expenses, how assessed.

To be a lien &c.

SEC. 6. It is hereby provided, if upon the publication of any improvement as hereinbefore in this chapter provided, any owner of any lot or real estate liable to be taxed therefor under this act, may perform, or cause to be performed at his own expense, such

Owners may perform work in lieu of tax.

part of such work for such improvement, under the direction of the supervisor or other person appointd for such purpose, as may amount to the sum for which the lot or lots owned by him shall be liable to be assessed, and any statement in writing by the supervisor or other person appointed as such for the time being, that such work has been performed, shall exempt such lot or lots on behalf of which such work has been performed from taxation for such improvement.

General provisions.

SEC. 7. The common council may make such further or other regulations for causing highways to be graded, levelled, gravelled, or cleaned, or to keep the same in repair, and for causing cross and side-walks, main drains, and sewers, or private drains to be constructed, laid, re-laid, removed, cleansed, and repaired as they may by ordinance ordain.

CHAHTER IX.

OF ASSESSMENTS AND COLLECTION OF TAXES.

Annual assessment, wehn to be made.

SECTION 1. Between the first day of May and the first day of August in each year, (unless further time shall be granted by the common council,) the assessors shall ascertain the names of all the taxable persons in the city and also all their taxable property, and all taxable estate therein on the first day of May of each year, and shall make out an assessment roll of all such taxable property, and appraise the same in he manner specified by the general laws of this state.

Notice of revision of assessment, how given.

SEC. 2. When such assessment roll shall be completed, the assessor shall give notice thereof in some newspaper published in the city, in which notice he shall fix some convenient time and place where he will be present for the purpose of hearing any objections of parties deeming themselves aggrieved by such assessment; and after such hearing the assessor shall make such alterations or revisions in such assessment roll as justice or equity may require.

Return, when to be made.

SEC. 3 Within two weeks after the day fixed by the assessor for the revision of the assessment roll as aforesaid, such assessor shall return such roll to the common council, which shall have power to supply omissions therein, and for the purpose of equalizing the same may alter, add to, take from, or otherwise correct and revise the same, provided the common council shall not have power to increase the aggregate amount of said roll except by the value of said property, real or personal, as may have been omitted by the assessor.

Councilmay equalize.

SEC. 4. When the assessment roll shall have been so revised and corrected or equalized by the common council, the same shall be confirmed by an order of the council and filed with the clerk. Thereupon the common council shall by resolution levy such sum or sums of money as may be sufficient for the several purposes for which taxes are herein authorized to be levied, which resolutions shall specify the various general purposes for which sums are levied.

When taxes to be a lien.

SEC. 5. All taxes and assessments, general or special, levied or assessed by the common council under this act, shall be a lien upon the real estate upon which the same may be imposed, voted, or assessed, for two years from and after the corrected assessment roll shall have been confirmed, and on personal estate from and after the delivery of the warrant for the collection thereof, until paid, and no sale or transfer shall affect the lien; and any personal property belonging to the debtor may be taken and sold for the payment of taxes on real or personal estate, or for highway tax, any law of this state to the contrary notwithstanding.

Personal property, when may be taken.

Clerk to issue warrant for taxes.

Sec. 6. The clerk shall issue a warrant for the taxes and shall attach such warrant to a book, in which book shall be ruled separate columns, in which the taxes levied, with five per cent. of the costs of collection, shall be respectively set down opposite of the name of the person or real estate subject thereto; and each column shall be headed with the name of the tax therein set down. All such warrants whether issued for the collection of general or special taxes and assessments, shall be signed by the mayor and clerk with the corporate seal thereto affixed, and the book to which the same is attached to be dessignated as the "tax list" shall contain true and perfected copies of the corrected assessment rolls upon which such warrants may be respectively issued, and such tax list with the warrant affixed, shall be delivered to the treasurer of the city for collection each year, within such time as the council may prescribe. A record of such delivery in the book kept for record of the proceedings of the common council, attested by the clerk, shall be sufficient evidence of such delivery.

What to be evidence of delivery of warrant.

Sec. 7. But such tax list before being delivered to the treasurer shall be compared by the clerk with the assessment roll as confirmed, and to it he shall append his certificate that the same has been compared by him, and that such tax list includes a true copy of said assessment roll, and of the whole thereof; and the said tax list when so certified shall be *prima facie* evidence in any court that the lands and persons therein named were subject to taxation, and that the assessment was just and equal.

List to be compared, and when to be evidence &c.

Sec. 8. Upon receipt of the tax list as aforesaid it shall be the duty of the treasurer of said city to give public notice in some newspaper printed in said city that such tax list has been committed to him for the purpose of collecting taxes therein, and that he will receive payment of taxes at his office in said city until the last Monday in February in each year, when the same will be returned to the county treasurer for collection, and the publication of such notice shall be deemed a demand, and a neglect to pay the taxes and assessments within the time specified shall be deemed a refusal to pay the same.

Treasurer to give notice of time of collection.

What deemed a demand and refusal.

Sec. 9. Returns of unpaid taxes, for all purposes

Annual returns to county treasurer, how made.

whatever in the city, shall annually be made by the city treasurer to the county treasurer, in the same manner as is, or may be provided by statute, in the case of unpaid town taxes, but the time of making such return shall be governed by this act.

Five per cent. to be repaid by county treasurer when collected.

SEC. 10. The five per cent. for costs of collection annually returned by the city treasurer upon unpaid taxes, shall be accounted for by the county treasurer, and repaid to the city when collected, in the same manner that other taxes are accounted for and repaid to the city; and no portion of such unpaid taxes, or five per cent. thereon returned, or interest thereon when collected, shall be retained by the county treasurer, either for his personal use or for the use of the county; but the fees allowed by law to the county treasurer for the collection of such unpaid taxes may be collected by such treasurer in addition to the whole sum returned.

County treasurer may collect his fees in addition.

Assessor, clerk and treasurer, when to be governed by statute.

SEC. 11. The assessor, clerk, and treasurer elected under this act shall severally have and possess the same powers, and be subject to the same duties and liabilities, as are or may be conferred or imposed upon such officers respectively by the laws of this state, except as otherwise specially provided in this act; *Provided, however*, That the common council shall have power by ordinance to prescribe the forms of assessment rolls, and more fully define the duties and liabilities of said officers, and make such rules and regulations respecting them as they may from time to time deem advisable.

Council may regulate assessments.

SEC. 12. The compensation of the city treasurer

shall not exceed a commission of two per cent. upon all moneys he shall pay out in his official capacity. Compensation of treasurer.

SEC. 13. No tax or assessment herein provided for shall become invalid by reason of any mere informality on the part of any officer in the discharge of his duties as herein or by general laws prescribed; and in case any real or personal estate in said city, justly and legally liable to taxation in any one year, by reason of any such informality, or of any accident or other cause may have been, or shall be legally discharged from the payment of any such just and equitable tax, whether for want of power to sell, to give deed, or other reason, the common council may on sufficient and conclusive evidence of such fact add the amount of such tax to the assessment roll of any succeeding year, whereupon the same shall be collected on such real or personal estate in the same manner as other taxes, and in the same manner as if no such informality, accident, or other cause had occurred. Assessments—when not invalid. Re-assessment, when may be made.

CHAPTER X.

OF FIRE DEPARTMENT.

SECTION 1. The common council, for the purpose of guarding against the calamities of fire, shall have power to prescribe the limits within which wooden buildings shall not be erected, or placed, or repaired, without the permission of the common council, and to direct that all and any buildings within the limits prescribed shall be made or constructed of fire proof material. Council may fix fire limits.

Sec. 2. The common council shall also have power:

May regulate stoves, fire-places, &c.

1st. To prevent the dangerous construction and condition of chimneys, fire-places, hearths, stoves, stove-pipes, ovens, boilers, and apparatus used in and about any building or manufactory, and to cause the same to be removed or placed in a safe and secure condition when considered dangerous.

May prevent deposit of ashes.

2d. To prevent the deposit of ashes, and to regulate and prevent the use of fire-works and fire-arms in unsafe places.

May regulate use of fire buckets

3d. To require the inhabitants to provide fire buckets, and to regulate the use of them.

May compel access to roof, &c.

4th. To compel the owners or occupants of buildings to have scuttles in the roofs, and stairs or ladders leading to the same.

May compel services at fires, &c.

5th. To compel such persons as they may deem proper to aid in the extinguishment of fires, and in the preservation of property exposed to danger thereat.

May secure dangerous buildings.

6th. To appoint one or more officers to enter into all buildings and enclosures, to discover whether the same are in a dangerous state, and to cause such as may be dangerous to be put in safe condition.

General powers.

7th. And generally to establish such regulations for the prevention and extinguishment of fires as the common council may deem expedient.

Fireengines—who to purchase and contral.

Sec. 3 The common council may procure fire engines, and other apparatus used for the extinguishment of fires, and have the charge and control of the same, and provide engine-houses, and other buildings necessary for preserving and safe-keeping the same.

Sec. 4. The common council may organize fire, hose, and hook and ladder companies, and appoint during pleasure a competent number of firemen to take the care and management of the engines, and other apparatus and implements used and provided for the extinguishment of fires; and may prescribe the duties of firemen, and make rules and regulations for their government, imposing reasonable fines and forfeitures for violating the same.

Fire companies; how organized.

Councilmay prescribe duties of.

Sec. 5. The common council may prescribe the duties of chief and assistant engineers of the fire department, who shall have the general care and management of such department.

Engineers; duties of.

Sec. 6. The firemen appointed under this act shall during their term of service as such, be exempt from serving on jurors in all courts of this state and be exempt from working on any highway tax.

Firemen; when exempt from jury duty and poll tax

Sec. 7. The name of each fireman shall be registered with the city clerk, and the evidence to entitle every such fireman to the exemptions provided in the preceeding section shall be the certificate of the clerk made within the year during which such exemption is claimed.

Fremen to be registered; certificate of clerk evidence of exemption.

CHAPTER XI.

OF THE BOARD OF EDUCATION.

SECTION 1. All that territory now lying within the corporate limits of the city of Kenosha, together with such territory as is hereinafter provided, shall constitute one school district, to be denominated, "city of Kenosha public school district."

Nome of school dist.

Boundaries.

Sec. 2. All that portion of territory lying in the town of Pleasant Prairie, adjoining the corporate limits of the city of Kenosha, and which is now annexed to the said city of Kenosha for school district purposes, shall continue to be so annexed for such purposes, and in like manner all that portion of territory lying in the town of Somers, adjoining the the city of Kenosha, and which is now annexed to the city of Kenosha for school district purposes, shall continue to be annexed for such purposes.

Vacancies how filled.

Sec. 3. The common council shall have power to fill any vacancy that may occur in the office of commissioner or superintendent of schools, and the person so appointed shall hold his office until the next ensuing election for said officers.

School commissioners, how may be removed.

Sec. 4. Any school commissioner may be removed from office for official misconduct by the common council, by a vote of two-thirds of the members thereof; but such commissioner shall be granted a full and fair hearing before being removed.

Corperate powers.

Sec. 5. The commissioners of schools of said city and the superintendent thereof shall constitute a board of education, which board shall be a corporate body in relation to all the powers and duties conferred upon them by virtue of this act; a majority of said board shall form a quorum for the transaction of business. At their first meeting after the annual election they shall elect one of their number President, and whenever the president shall be absent or unable

Election of president.

to serve, a president pro tem. may be appointed. The superintendent of schools shall be clerk of the board of education, unless he shall be absent or unable to serve, in which case the board may appoint a clerk pro tem. No member of the board of education, except the clerk shall be allowed any compensation for any of the services prescribed in this act; the clerk shall receive such compensation as may be agreed upon by the board.

Superintendent to be clerk of school board.

Sec. 6. The clerk shall keep a record of the proceedings of said board of education, which record, or a transcript thereof, certified by the said clerk and president, shall be received in all courts as *prima facie* evidence of the facts therein set forth.

Record of proceedings

When to be evidence.

Sec. 7. The common council shall have power and it shall be their duty to raise, on or before the first Monday of September in each year, by tax on the real and personal estate in said district, such sum or sums as may be recommended by the board of education to be necessary or proper for any of the following purposes:

Annual tax; how to be raised.

1st. To purchase, lease, or improve sites for school houses.

2d. To build, purchase, lease, enlarge, alter, improve, and repair school houses, and their out houses and appurtenances.

3d. To purchase, improve, and repair school apparatus, books, furniture and appendages.

4th. To procure fuel and defray the contingent expenses of the schools and the district library.

5th. To pay the wages of teachers, due after the application of the public moneys, which may by law be appropriated and provided for that purpose.

6th. To provide for the payment of any indebtedness which may have been lawfully incurred by said district.

Liabilities. Sec. 8. All debts and liabilities legally incurred, or contracts legally entered into heretofore, by the district board of district number one, of the city of Kenosha, shall be assumed and carried out by the board of education the same as the district board would have been required to do had this act not have been passed. The common council shall cause the taxes provided for in this act to be levied and collected annually on all such real and personal property, or capital of any kind within the limits of said district, as is subject to taxation by the laws of this state for general purposes; and said taxes shall be collected in the same manner as the annual taxes of said city are levied and collected.

Taxes, how levied and collected.

Sec. 9. All moneys raised in pursuance of the provisions of this act shall be paid into the city treasury, and it shall be the duty of the treasurer of said city to apply for and receive from the county treasurer all moneys that may come into the hands of the said county treasurer from the state school fund apportioned to said district; and also all moneys that may come into the said county treasurer's hands from other sources for school purposes and belonging to said district. And the said city treasurer shall be

City treasurer to receive and disburse school moneys.

liable to the same penalties for any official misconduct in relation to any school moneys which may come into his hands in like manner as for moneys belonging to the city of Kenosha. The said city treasurer shall be allowed not exceeding one half of one per cent. for receiving and distributing the moneys which may come into his hands from the state school fund, apportioned to said district. His compensation.

Sec. 10. The city treasurer shall not pay out any of the moneys in his hands received from the state or county for school purposes, or any money levied and collected by any of the provisions of this act, except by an order drawn upon him, signed by the president and clerk of the board; *Provided,* That no such order shall be drawn except by virtue of a resolution of said board. Treasurer to pay no money without order.

Sec. 11. The board of education shall have power, and it shall be their duty as follows: Specific powers of board.

1st. To establish and organize such and so many schools in said city, in addition to the schools now established therein, as they shall deem necessary. May establish schools.

2d. To purchase or hire school houses, rooms, and lots, or sites for school houses, and to improve the same. May improve houses.

3d. Upon such lots or sites, and upon any lots now occupied for school purposes, to build, enlarge, alter, improve and repair school houses, out-houses, and appurtenances, as they may deem necessary and proper. May repair or build structures.

May provide books, fuel, &c. 4th. To purchase books for indigent children, to purchase and repair school apparatus, furniture, and appendages, to provide fuel for the schools, and to defray their contingent expenses, and the expenses of the district library.

May keep furniture and appendages. 5th. To have the custody and safe-keeping of the school houses, out-houses, books, furniture, and appendages, and to see that the ordinances of the city council in relation thereto are enforced.

May contract with and remove teachers. 6th. To contract with and employ all teachers in the schools who shall have been licensed by the superintendent of schools, and to remove such teachers when they shall deem it necessary.

May pay teachers' wages. 7th. To pay the wages of teachers out of the school moneys which shall have been apportioned to or received by said city, so far as the same shall be sufficient, and the residue thereof from any moneys authorized to be raised for that purpose by the provisions of this act.

May alter and modify school regulations. 8th. To adopt, alter, modify, and repeal from time to time, as they may deem expedient, such rules and regulations for the organization, government and instruction of schools as they may deem necessary; to regulate the reception of pupils, their graduation into classes, and the transfer of pupils, from one school to another, and generally to promote the good order and welfare of the schools.

May report to council necessary regulations for protection of houses and grounds. 9th. To prepare and report to the common council such ordinances and regulations as may be necessary for the protection, safe-keeping, care and preservation of school houses, lots, fences, shade trees, and other appurtenances, and all property connected with and appertaining to the schools; and to suggest proper penalties for the violation of such ordinances and regulations.

10th. To determine and certify to the common council on or before the first Monday of August in each year the sum in their opinion necessary to be raised for school purposes under the provisions of this act, specifying the sum required for each of the purposes therein mentioned.

May certify to council annual sum to be raised.

Sec. 12. The said board of education shall have power to allow the children of persons not resident within the district to attend the schools in said city which are under the control of said board, upon such terms as the said board shall by resolution prescribe, fixing the tuition that shall be paid for such attendance.

Non-resident scholars; how may be admitted.

Sec. 13. The said board shall have the care and direction of the school district library, and they shall have power to disburse any moneys appropriated by any law of this state for school libraries; it shall be their duty to provide a library room and appoint a librarian, and make regulations in respect to such library as they shall deem expedient; they may also remove from such library all such books as they may deem of an improper character to be read by children of the district.

Librarian; who to appoint, &c.

Sec. 14. It shall be the duty of said board of education, at least fifteen days before the annual election on the first Tuesday of April, to prepare and

Board to make annual report.

report to the common council a true and correct statement of the receipts and disbursements under and in pursuance of the provisions of this act, during the preceeding year, in which statement shall be mentioned under appropriate heads, as follows:

1st. The amount of school moneys received from the state school fund.

2d. The amount of moneys received arising from county taxes for school purposes.

3d. The amount of moneys received from the school district taxes levied for school purposes.

4th. All other moneys received by the city treasurer for school purposes, specifying the sources.

5th. the manner in which the moneys drawn from the city treasurer for school purposes have been expended, specifying the amount paid for each expenditure under appropriate heads.

When board subject to rules of state superintendent.

Sec. 15. The said board of education shall be subject from time to time to the rules and regulations made by the state superintendent of schools, so far as the same may be applicable and not inconsistent with the provisions of this act.

City superintendent to examine teachers.

Sec. 16. The city superintendent shall examine all teachers making application to teach in the public schools of said city, which examinations shall be made in presence of the board of education, if desired by said board; all certificates granted by said superintendent shall be in form as prescribed by the state superintendent. The said city superintendent shall visit the schools at least twice during each

School visitations, when to be made.

term, and report their condition to the board of education, with such suggestions for their improvement as he may deem proper, immediately after the close of each term; he shall also make such suggestions to the said board as he may deem necessary for improving and repairing the school houses, grounds, fences and appurtenances thereunto belonging. The amount of the superintendent's compensation shall be determined by the board of education. Compensation.

Sec. 17 The city superintendent shall, betweenthe first and fifteenth days of October,in each year,make and transmit to the clerk of the board of supervisors a report in writing, bearing date the first day of October in each year of its transmission, which report shall in form be such as is now by law required to be made annually by town superintendents of schools, and transmitted to the said clerk. Superintendent to report to clerk of board of supervisors.

Sec. 18. The common council shall have power to pass such ordinances and regulations as the board of education may report as necessary and proper for the protection and safe-keeping, care, and preservation of the school houses, lots, appurtenances, and all property belonging to and appertaining to the schools; and also to impose proper penalties for the violation thereof; all such penalties shall be collected in the same manner as the penalties for a violation of a city ordinance, and when so collected shall be paid to the treasurer of said city, and be subject to the board of education in the same manner as other moneys raised pursuant to the provisions of this act. Council may provide by ordinance for protection of school houses and grounds. Penalties, how collected.

Title to buildings, lot, &c., in whom vested. liability, &c.

Sec. 19. The title to all school houses, lots, furniture, books, apparatus, and appurtenances shall be vested in the city of Kenosha, and the same while used or appropriated for school purposes shall not be levied upon or sold by virtue of any warrant or execution for the payment of any debt contracted, or liability incurred, except for school purposes, nor shall the same be subject to taxation for any purpose whatever. And the said city in its corporate capacity shall have power to take, hold and dispose of any real or personal estate, transferred to it by gift, grant, bequest, or devise, for the use of the public schools of said district.

Funds; by whom to be held.

Sec. 20. All moneys required to be raised by the provisions of this act, on being raised as herein provided, shall be held by the treasurer of the city of Kenosha, and by him placed to the credit of the board of education, and shall be drawn out in pursuance of a resolution of said board, by orders drawn by the president and countersigned by the clerk of said board, payable to the order of the person or persons entitled to receive such moneys; and the said treasurer shall keep the funds authorized by this act to be received by him, separate and distinct from any funds that he is or may by law be authorized to receive.

Their disposition, &c.

When city clerk to deliver statement to town clerks of taxes levied, &c.

Sec. 21. The city clerk shall, on or before the fourth Monday in November in each year, deliver to the town clerk of any town adjoining the city of Kenosha, in which there shall be any part of district or territory annexed to the public school district of said city, a statement in writing verified by his affidavit, showing the whole amount of taxes levied by the common council for the current year, for school purposes authorized by this act; such statement shall contain a list of all corporations and descriptions of property liable to a school district tax, together with the proportion of tax to be assessed in any such part of district or territory annexed as aforesaid. Such proportion shall be ascertained from the valuations contained in the last assessment roll of such town, and to enable the city clerk to ascertain the same, the town clerk of each town shall, on demand at any time after he has received the assessment of his town for that year, deliver to the city clerk a certified statement of the valuations of real and personal property in that part of district or territory annexed to the said city for the purpose aforementioned.

Townclerks—when to deliver to city clerk statement of valuation

Sec. 22. The town clerk receiving the statement mentioned in the last preceeding section shall assess such tax, or the due proportion thereof upon the real and personal property liable thereto, placing the same in a separate column in the assessment roll of his town, delivered to the town treasurer for collection; and such tax shall be collected or returned in all respects as other taxes, and when collected the money shall be paid over to the treasurer of the city of Kenosha.

Duty of town clerk.

taxes how collected and paid.

Boundaries of district; how altered or regulated

Sec. 23. Whenever it shall be necessary and expedient to add any additional territory to the Kenosha public school district, from any adjoining town, or to set off any territory annexed, or to alter the boundaries of any such territory, the town superintendent of any such town to be affected by such annexation, alteration or setting off, and the superintendent of the city of Kenosha, shall meet together, and when so met, shall possess the same powers as are now by law conferred on town superintendents of adjoining towns, to make such regulations and alterations of boundaries as may be deemed necessary and proper.

CHAPTER XII.

OF RAILROAD COMMISSIONER.

Commissioner to be director.

SECTION 1. The railroad commissioner shall be *ex officio* a member of the board of directors of the Kenosha and Beloit raliroad company, with all the duties, responsibilities and power incident to the office of director under the charter of said railroad company.

Commissioner to vote on city stock.

Sec. 2. It shall be the duty of said commissioner to attend all meetings of the stockholders of the Kenosha and Beloit rail road company, and to vote in person, the same as any individual stockholder, on all shares of stock held by the city of Kenosha in the stock of said company.

Sec. 3. The railroad commissioner shall have generally the charge and control of all interests the city of Kenosha now has or may hereafter have in the Kenosha and Beloit railroad. He shall receive all funds paid into the hands of the city treasurer on account of the tax for the benefit of the Kenosha and Beloit railroad company, and shall hereafter redeem all scrip which has been issued to said railroad company, as the same becomes due, making such provisions therefor, or recommending such measures to the common council as he may deem necessary for the benefit of the tax payers of the city. General duties.

CHAPTER XIII.

OF LEGAL PROCEEDINGS.

Section 1. All actions brought to recover any penalty or forfeiture incurred under this act, or under the ordinances, by-laws, or police regulations made in pursuance of it, shall be brought in the corporate name. It shall be lawful to declare generally in debt for such penalty or forfeiture, stating the clause of this act, the by-laws, ordinances or regulations under which the penalty or forfeiture is claimed, and to give the special matter in evidence under it. Suits to be brought in name of city. Declaration how made.

When process to be by warrant.

Sec. 2. In all suits for any violation of any ordinance, by-law, police or other regulation, the first process may be by warrant.

Jurisdiction of justices.

Sec. 3. Either of the justices of the peace in said city shall have jurisdiction in any action for the recovery of any fine or penalty not exceeding one hundred dollars, under this act, or any ordinance, by-law, or police regulation of the common council, anything in the laws of this state to the contrary notwithstanding; and either of said justices shall have power to fine or imprison, or both, in their discretion, where such discretion may be vested in them by any such ordinance or regulation, or by this act.

Execution, when to issue; defendant when may be imprisoned.

Sec. 4. Execution may issue immediately on the rendition of judgment, and if the defendant in any such action have no goods or chattels, lands or tenements whereof the judgment can be collected, the execution may require the defendant to be imprisoned in the jail of Kenosha county for such term, not exceeding sixty days, as may be prescribed by ordinance.

Costs, by whom to be paid.

Sec. 5. All costs incurred in prosecuting for the recovery of any penalty or forfeiture, and all such penalties or forfeitures under this act or any ordinance, by-law, or regulation of the city, when collected for the use of the city, shall be paid to the treasurer.

Who deemed an incompetent witness.

Sec. 6. No person shall be an incompetent justice, commissioner, witness, or juror by reason of his being an inhabitant or free-holder in the city of Kenosha, in any action or proceeding in which the said city shall be a party in interest.

Sec. 7. A printed copy of an ordinance, by-law, or resolution purporting to be printed by authority of the common council shall be *prima facie* evidence in any court of its due passage and publication, and may be received in evidence. Printed copies, when evidence.

Sec. 8. This act shall be deemed a public act, and may be read in evidence without proof; and judicial notice shall be taken thereof in all courts and places. Charter to be evidence without proof.

Sec. 9. All officers of the city created conservators of the peace by this act shall have power to arrest, or cause to be arrested, with or without process, all persons who shall break, or threaten to break the peace, or to violate any city ordinance or police regulation; commit for examination, and if necessary detain such persons in custody over night in the county jail or other safe place, and shall have and exercise such other powers as conservators of the peace as the common council may prescribe. Peace officers, when may arrest with or without process.

Sec. 10. No penalty or judgment recovered in favor of the city shall be remitted or discharged without a vote of two-thirds of all the aldermen elect. Penalties, how remitted.

Sec. 11. Whenever any suit or action shall be commenced against said city, the service thereof may be made by leaving a copy of the process by the proper officer with the mayor or clerk, whose duty it shall be forthwith to inform the council thereof, or take such other proceeding as by the ordinances and resolutions of said council may in such case be provided. Process against the city to be served on mayor or clerk—their duties.

CHAPTER XIV.

MISCELLANEOUS PROVISIONS.

Existing ordinances to be of force till repealed

Section 1. All ordinances, regulations, and resolutions now in force in the city of Kenosha, and not inconsistent with this act, until altered shall remain in force under this act until altered, amended, or repealed by the common council after this act shall take effect.

Actions, rights, &c., to survive, &c.

Sec. 2. All actions, rights, fines, penalties, forfeitures, in suit or otherwise, which have accrued under the several acts consolidated herein, shall survive to and be vested in and prosecuted by the corporation hereby created.

Property vested in new corporation.

Sec 3. All property, real, personal, or mixed, belonging to the city of Kenosha, is hereby vested in the corporotion created by this act.

Officers to hold over their full term.

Sec. 4. All officers of the city of Kenosha now in office shall respectively continue in the same for the several terms for which they were elected or appointed; but shall be governed in their official action by this act after it shall take effect.

Act not to effect any proceeding had before it shall take effect.

Sec. 5. This act shall not invalidate any legal act done before this act shall take effect by the common council of the city of Kenosha or by the officers of said city; nor divest their successors under this act of any rights of property or liability which may have accrued to, or been created by said corporation prior to the passage of this act.

SEC. 6. No general laws of this state contravening the provisions of this act shall be considered as repealing, amending, or modifying the same, unless such purpose be expressly set forth in such laws. General laws of state in contravention must be express.

SEC. 7. "An act to incorporate the city of Kenosha, approved February 8th, 1850;" "An act to extend the corporate limits of the city of Kenosha, approved February 17th, 1851,;" An act to amend an act to incorporate the city of Kenosha, approved March 8, 1851;" "An act to amend an act entitled an act to incorporate the city of Kenosha, approved March 19th, 1852;" "An act to amend the charter of the city Kenosha, approved March 23d, 1853;" and all other acts of the legislature of this state, so far as each or either of them conflict with this act are hereby repealed. Repealing clauses.

SEC. 8. This act shall take effect from and after its passage. When act to take effect.

Approved March 2d, 1857.

AMENDMENTS TO THE CITY CHARTER.

The people of the State of Wisconsin, represented in senate and assembly, do enact as follows:

Third ward boundaries.

SECTION 1. The city of Kenosha is hereby divided into four wards, as follows: All that part of the city lying south of the township line, between towns one and two, shall constitute the third ward. All that part of the city lying north of the third ward, as herein constituted, and south of a line drawn through the centre of Pearl street, continued to the east and west boundaries of the city, shall constitute the first ward. All that part of the city lying north of the first ward, as herein constituted, and south of the following described line, viz: A line commencing on the eastern boundary line of the city, at a point due east of the north line of lot number twenty-two in block number one, on Washington Island, thence to and along said north line of lot twenty-two to Washington street; thence to and along the center of Middle street on said island, and across Pike creek to the center of the alley north of, and adjoining to lot number five in block number seventy-four, and along the centre of said alley to Main street, thence westerly to the centre of Middle street, and along the centre of Middle street to the centre of the creek, and thence

First ward boundaries.

Fourth ward boundaries.

along the centre of said creek, north-westerly to the western boundary of the city, shall constitute the fourth ward. And all that part of the city lying north of the fourth ward as herein constituted, shall constitute the second ward. Second ward boundaries.

SEC. 2. At the annual election to be holden in said city on the first Tuesday in April, 1858, and annually thereafter, there shall be elected by the qualified electors of each ward, three aldermen for such ward, who shall hold their office for the term of one year, and until their successors shall be duly elected and qualified; and from and after such election and qualification the common council shall consist of the mayor and aldermen from each ward, elected as herein provided; *Provided,* That no alderman shall receive any compensation whatever for his services as alderman, nor be interested, directly or indirectly, in any contract made with the city. Aldermen when and how elected and term of office. To have no compensation—not to contract &c. &c.

SEC. 3. At the next annual election in said city there shall be elected in each ward, by the qualified electors thereof, two school commissioners for each ward, one for the term of one, and one for the term of two years, which term shall be expressed upon the ballot voted by such elector, and the person receiving the highest number of votes "for school commissioner for one year," shall be declared duly elected to such office for the term of one; and the person receiving the highest number of votes "for school commissioner for two years," shall be declared duly elected for two years; aud there shall be annually there- School commissioners, when and how elected. Term of office.

after elected, by the qualified electors of each ward one school commissioner for such ward who shall hold his office for the term of two years. The school commissioners elected under the provisions of this act, shall have and exercise all the rights, powers, and duties conferred upon school commissioners by the act to which this is amendatory.

Powers and duties.

County supervisors, when and how elected

SEC. 4. At the first meeting of the common council elected under the provisions of this act, and at the first meeting of the common council in each year thereafter, the aldermen shall proceed to elect by ballot from their own number three supervisors, no two of whom shall be aldermen from the same ward.—Each supervisor shall be elected upon a separate vote, and the aldermen receiving the highest number of votes on each of such ballotings, shall be, for the year then next ensuing, members of the board of supervisors of the county of Kenosha, and shall have and exercise all the rights and powers now or hereafter conferred by law upon other members of the county board. The mayor and city clerk shall issue to the persons elected supervisors certficates of their election, which certificates shall be sufficient evidence thereof; *Provided, however*, That in case of a failure to elect such supervisors, or either of them, at the first annual meeting, or in case a vacancy should occur in the office of supervisor, the aldermen may proceed to elect a supervisor or supervisors; at a regular meeting of the common council, fixed upon at some prior meeting thereof.

Rights and powers.

Provision on failure to elect.

SEC. 5. At special elections hereafter to be held in said city, at which all the qualified electors of said city may be entitled to vote, one poll only shall be required to be held in said city, in case the common council shall deem the same to be expedient and so direct. In such case such poll shall be opened and held in the first ward, and shall in all respects be conducted in the same manner as other city elections, and shall have the same validity as if the same had been held in the several wards.

Special election, how may be conducted and held.

SEC. 6. Section nine of chapter two of the act to which this act is amendatory, and so much of said act as conflicts with the provisions of this act, is hereby repealed.

Repealing clause.

SEC. 7. This act shall take effect and be in force from and after its passage.

When act to take effect.

AN ACT to provide for the appointment of Superintendent of Public Schools in the city of Kenosha.

The people of the State of Wisconsin, represented in Senate and Assembly, do enact as follows:

SECTION 1. That from and after the expiration of the present term for which the superintendent of public schools of the city of Kenosha was elected, such office shall be filled by appointment by the board of school commissioners of said city, and the powers and duties and the tenure of office of said superintendent shall be the same as now provided by law.

Superintendent of schools.

Repealed. SEC. 2. All acts and parts of acts amendatory to the charter of the city of Kenosha, contravening the provisions of this act, are hereby repealed.

SEC. 3. This act shall be in force and take effect from and after its passage.

Approved March 17, 1859.

AN ACT to amend an act, entitled an act to amend an act entitled "an act to consolidate and amend the act to incorporate the city of Kenosha, and the several acts amendatory thereof."

The people of the State of Wisconsin, represented in Senate and assembly, do enact as follows:

Amendm'nt in reference to supervisors. SECTION 1. Section four of chapter 3, of the private and local laws of 1858, entitled an act to amend an act, entitled "an act to consolidate and amend the act to incorporate the city of Kenosha, and the several acts amendatory thereof," is hereby amended by striking out the word "three" where it occurs in the fifth line of said section, and inserting the word "four," so as to read "four supervisors," instead of three.

SEC. 2. This act shall take effect and be in force from and after its passage.

Approved March 22, 1860.

AN ACT to amend article 28 of section 8, in chapter 5 of chapter 183, of the private and local laws of 1857, entitled "an act to consolidate and amend the act to incorporate the city of Kenosha, and the several acts amendatory thereto."

The people of the State of Wisconsin, represented in senate and assembly, do enact as follows:

SECTION 1. Article 28 of section 8, in chapter five of chapter 133 of the private and local laws of 1857, entitled "an act to consolidate and amend the act to incorporate the city of Kenosha, and the several acts amendatory thereto," is hereby amended so as to read as follows: "28th. To have the privilege of using the jail of the county of Kenosha for the imprisonment of offenders against the ordinances, rules or by-laws; and all persons so imprisoned shall be in the custody of the Sheriff of the county: *provided*, that the sheriff's fees, and all other expenses, shall be paid by the said city of Kenosha, and the county of Kenosha shall not be liable to pay the same, or any part thereof."

Offenders against ordinances &c., may be confined in county jail.

Approved April 2, 1862.

AN ACT to amend the charter of the city of Kenosha.

The people of the State of Wisconsin, represented in senate and assembly, do enact as follows:

SECTION 1. The 10th section of chapter 9 of chapter 133 of the private and local laws of 1857, is hereby amended, so as to read as follows: "The five per cent. for costs of collection annually returned by the city treasurer upon all unpaid state and county taxes, together with the interest on said taxes until the lands on which said taxes are levied shall be sold, or the taxes otherwise collected, shall be retained by the county treasurer for the benefit of the county, and no portion of said five per cent. and interest shall be repaid to the city; and of the five per cent.

Account of the 5 per cent. costs.

for costs of collection, annually returned by the city treasurer upon all other unpaid taxes, two per cent, shall be retained by the county treasurer, for the use of the county; and the remaining three per cent., together with the interest on such unpaid taxes, shall be accounted for by the county treasurer and repaid to the city when collected, in the same manner that other taxes are accounted for and repaid to the city.

SEC. 2. This act shall take effect and be in force from and after its passage and publication.

Approved March 20, 1865.

AN ACT to amend an act entitled "an act to consolidate and amend the act to incorporate the city of Kenosha, and the several acts amendatory thereto," approved March 2d, 1857.

The people of the State of Wisconsin, represented in senate and assembly, do enact as follows:

Amendments.

SECTION 1. Section two of chapter seven of an act entitled "an act to consolidate and amend the act to incorporate the city of Kenosha, and the several acts amendatory thereto," approved March 2d, 1857, is hereby amended, by adding after the word "highways," where the same first occurs in said section, the words "streets, alleys;" also, by inserting the same words in the singular number where they subsequently occur in the reading of said section, after the word "highway."

When council may order opening &c. of streets.

SEC. 2. Section nine of said chapter seven is also further amended, by adding thereto the words "but upon satisfactory proof of such tender or deposit having been made, the common council shall, except in case of the appeal provided for in sections eleven and twelve of said chapter, make such order for the immediate opening, altering, widening, improving straightening or vacating such highways, streets, alleys or public grounds, as may seem expedient."

SEC. 3. This act shall take effect and be in force from and after its passage and publication.

Approved April 6, 1865.

RULES

OF THE

COMMON COUNCIL.

RULES OF THE COMMON COUNCIL.

Duty of the mayor.

1st. The mayor, or presiding officer, shall at the appointed hour of meeting call the city council to order; and if a quorum be present, he shall direct the minutes of the preceeding meeting to be read, corrected if necessary, and approved. It shall be the duty of the mayor, or presiding officer, to preserve order and decorum, and to decide all questions of order, subject to an appeal to the common council.

Order of business.

2d. The order of business, after the reading of the minutes, shall be as follows;

1. The presentation of petitions.
2. The reports of standing committees.
3. Reports of select committees.
4. Communications to the common council.
5. Unfinished business of preceding meetings.

Rule in regard to motions.

3d. When a motion is made and seconded, it shall be stated by the presiding officer, or read by the clerk, previous to being debated or acted upon by the common council. If any member require it, all motions (except to adjourn, postpone, or commit) shall be reduced to writing: any motion may be withdrawn, by consent of the common council, before discussion or amendment.

Members shall vote unless excused, &c.

4th. Every member present when a question is put shall vote, unless the common council shall, from some special cause, excuse him or unless he shall be directly interested in the question ; in which case he shall not vote.

In regard to adjournment and previous question.

5th. A motion to adjourn shall always be considered in order, and, together with a call for the previous question, shall be decided without debate.

Duty of members in speaking.

6th. When any member is about to speak in debate, or make report of any matter to the common council, he shall rise from his seat and address himself to the presiding officer, and shall confine himself to the subject matter under consideration, and avoid personalities.

Chair to decide in certain case.

7th. When two or more members rise to speak at once, the presiding officer shall name the member who is first to speak.

Restriction in speaking.

8th. No member shall speak except in his place, nor more than twice on any question, except on leave of the common council.

Speaker not to be interrupted.

9th. When a member is speaking no member shall entertain any private discourse, or in any way interrupt the speaker, except as to a question of order.

Division of question.

10th. Any member may call for a division of a question, when the same will admit thereof.

Filling of blanks.

11th. When a blank is to be filled, and different sums or times proposed, the question shall first be put upon the largest sum and longest time.

Privileged questions.

12th. When a question is under debate, no motion shall be received unless to adjourn, to lay on the table, for the previous question, to postpone to a day certain, to commit, to amend, or to postpone indefinitely; and these several motions shall have precedence in the order in which they stand arranged.

13th. The previous question shall be admitted on demand of any member, and until decided shall preclude all amendments and discussion. Previous question.

14th. It shall be competent for any member, when a question is taken, to call for the ayes and noes, which shall be recorded by the clerk. Ayes and noes.

15th. In all cases when a resolution or a motion shall be entered on the minutes, the name of the member moving the same shall also be entered on the minutes. Name of member to be entered.

16th. Standing or select committees shall always report in writing. Reports to be made in writing.

17th. A majority of the members of the common council shall constitute a quorum for the transaction of business, but no ordinance shall be passed, or appropriation of money voted, unless eight members shall vote in favor thereof. Quorum.

18th. It shall require a vote of two-thirds of the members present to suspend any rule of the city council. Suspension of rules.

19th No ordinance shall be passed, or account allowed, or appropriation made, without first having been proposed or considered at a previous meeting. Ordinances and accounts.

20th. The following standing committees, to consist of three members each, shall be elected by a majority of this council: Standing committees

1. On Finance.
2. " Claims.
3. " Harbor and bridges.
4. " Fire department.
5. " Police.
6. " Judiciary.
7. " Printing.
8. " Public grounds.
9. " Streets and alleys.
10 " Pauper affairs.

Reports, how addressed. 21st. All reports of committees shall be addressed to the mayor and common council of the city of Kenosha.

ORDINANCES

OF THE

CITY OF KENOSHA.

REVISED ORDINANCES.

ORDINANCE NO. I.

OF POLICE OFFICERS AND THEIR DUTIES.

SECTION 1. *Be it ordained by the common council of the city of Kenosha:* The mayor, aldermen, marshal, constables and such special constables or watchmen as the council may appoint, or authorize to be appointed, shall constitute the police of this city; and it shall be the duty of each of them to arrest, or cause to be arrested, and taken before any justice of the peace of said city, and to complain of and prosecute any person who shall violate any ordinance, or any portion of any ordinance of said city; and whenever any justice cannot conveniently be found, or whenever any such arrest shall be made after the hour of seven o'clock in the evening, may commit any person so arrested to the county jail, or otherwise detain such person in custody for a time not exceeding twenty-four hours, when such person so arrested may be brought before any justice of the peace of said city and dealt with according to law.

Who shall be police.

Offenders, when may be committed by police.

SEC. 2. The marshal, any constable, special constable or watchman who shall refuse or wilfully neglect to perform any of the duties required of him by

Penalty for neglect of duty.

this ordinance, or by the city charter, shall be liable to prosecution therefor, before any justice of the peace of said city, and upon conviction thereof shall forfeit and pay a penalty of not exceeding twenty dollars for each offence, and in default of the payment thereof shall be imprisoned in the county jail not exceeding twenty days.

Penalty for resisting officers.

SEC. 3. If any person shall resist any police officer or any other officer of this city in the discharge of his duties; or if any person, being roquested, shall refuse to assist any police officer in arresting any person for any offence committed against any ordinance of this city; or if any person under arrest shall attempt to escape from the custody of any police officer he shall forfeit and pay a penalty of not less than ten dollars, and in default thereof shall be imprisoned in the county jail twenty days.

GEO. H. PAUL, *Mayor.*

Passed February 20, 1858.

H. T. WEST, *City Clerk.*

ORDINANCE NO. II.

OF THE DUTIES OF MARSHAL, CLERK, AND TREASURER.

Marshal, to prosecute &c.

SECTION 1. *Be it ordained by the common council of the city fo Kenosha:* The marshal shall see that all the ordinances, orders, and resolutions of the common council are enforced; he shall prosecute offenders before any justice of the city, in the name and on behalf of the city, and procure evidence in all prosecutions in which the city shall be interested; he shall see that all orders of the board of health are promptly executed; he shall attend to the collection of all fines, penalties, and licenses; he shall deposit all moneys collected by him immediately with the city treasury, taking duplicate receipts for the same, and depositing one of them with the clerk; he shall remove or abate all nuisances or causes of disease within the limits of the city which may come to his knowledge; he shall give personal or written notice to all members of the council of special meetings called by the mayor; he shall attend all meetings of the common council, and shall provide for lights, fuel, fire, and such other convenience for the council, and in all other matters not herein specified shall be subject to the order of the mayor or common council; *Provided*, however, that in no case shall he incur any expense to the city in the discharge of any duty without the consent of the mayor or of the common council.

Shall abate nuisances.

Proviso.

Sec. 2. the clerk shall keep a complete record of the proceedings of the council; he shall engross all ordinances, orders and by-laws, in a separate book to be kept for that purpose, and furnish copies of the same for publication: he shall issue orders on the treasurer for such appropriations as may be made by the common council, and shall keep a

Clerk to keep records and accounts.

distinct and classified account of such appropriations; he shall keep on file all papers belonging to the city, including receipts of the treasurer for all moneys paid into the treasury and for all tax lists delivered to him; he shall issue certificates of all licenses granted and keep a record of the same; he shall compare all returns to the common council by the treasurer with the stubs of orders issued, and with the receipts of the treasurer for moneys paid in, cancelling the orders under the direction of the finance committee, and preserving them on file not less than one year; and at the close of each fiscal year he shall report to the council, and if by it approved, shall publish a detailed statement of the receipts and expenditure of the city for the year, including, so far as he may be able to ascertain, the amount of outstanding dues to and from the city.

Shall file papers, and issue licenses.

Shall make annual statement.

When treasurer not to pay money

Sec. 3. The treasurer shall pay no money from the treasury except an order be drawn upon him for amounts appropriated, in substantially the following form.

No.———	$ *City Order.* No.———
	KENOSHA,————18—.
$	The Treasurer of the City of Kenosha will pay to
Date.	————————, or order, ————dollars
To———	out of any funds in the treasury belonging to the
	city; the same having been allowed for————
For———	————*Clerk.* ————*Mayor.*

Shall make

He shall return to the common council as often as

once in three months all the orders he may have received previous to the last return, with a schedule of the same and of moneys paid in; he shall receipt to the clerk all tax lists which may be placed in his hands for collection, and furnish the marshal, or other proper officer, with duplicate receipts for all other moneys paid into his hands as treasurer.

quarterly report.

Shall furnish receipt to marshal.

GEO. H. PAUL, *Mayor.*

Passed March 24, 1858.

H. T. WEST, *City Clerk.*

ORDINANCE NO. III.

AN ORDINANCE RELATING TO HARBOR MASTER.

SECTION 1. *Be it ordained by the common council of the city of Kenosha:* The common council may once in each year or oftener appoint a harbor master, who shall hold his office for the term of one year and until his successor is appointed, unless sooner removed by the council..

Council may appoint harbor master.

Sec 2. The harbor master is hereby authorized and required to give such orders and directions relative to the location, change of place or station, manner of moving, or use of the harbor, of every vessel, craft or float, lying, moving, or laid up in the harbor, as may be necessary to promote good order therein, and the safety and equal convenience of such vessels, crafts or floats; and any owner, master, or other person

Duties and powers of harbor master.

having charge of the same who shall refuse or neglect to obey any such order or direction, shall be subject to a penalty of twenty-five dollars for every such neglect or refusal; which penalty shall constitute a lien upon such vessel, craft or float, until fully paid.

Penalty.

GEO. H. PAUL, *Mayor.*

Passed March 24, 1858.

H. T. WEST, *City Clerk*

ORDINANCE NO. IV.

RELATING TO KENOSHA CEMETERY AND CITY SEXTON.

Boundaries of cemetery.

SECTION 1. *Be it ordained by the common council of the city of Kenosha:* That part of N. E. ¼ of section six, town one, range twenty-three, deeded to the town of Southport by R. H. Deming and Charles Durkee for a burial ground, and also that part of said section platted out by Josiah Bond as a burial place, shall be known and distinguished as "Kenosha Cemetery," and shall be used only as a place of burial.

Clerk to keep plat &c

SEC. 2. A copy of the present plat of said cemetery now on file in the office of the register of deeds of Kenosha county, shall be kept in the office of the city clerk; and all lots, blocks, or halves of blocks in said cemetery owned by the city, shall be sold by the mayor and clerk of this city who may give deeds for the same, whenever application shall be made according to the plan of said plat, at such prices as are hereinafter fixed.

Sec. 3. The prices of lots, blocks or halves of blocks, in said cemetery, are hereby fixed as follows: 13, 15, 17, 24, 25, 27, 29, 35, 37, 39, 41, 43, 44, 45, 52, 53, 54, 56, 58, 60, 67, 69, 71, 73, 86, 88, 90, 92 and 94 at twenty-five dollars for each block; each half block in said blocks at fourteen dollars; each single lot in said blocks at eight dollars; all lots remaining unsold in blocks 46, 51 and 84 at eight dollars each; blocks 8 and 10 at thirty dollars each, and lots 1 and 2 in said blocks 8 and 10 at 10 dollars each; lots 3 and 4 respectively in said blocks 8 & 10 at 8 dollars each, if sold separately, but if sold in half blocks, the north half of each block at sixteen dollars, and the south half of each block at fourteen dollars; block 64 at thirty dollars, and the south half of block 49 at nine dollars. Prices of lots and blocks.

Sec. 4. The blocks in said cemetry from No. 95 to 101 inclusive are hereby set apart as a free burial ground; *Provided*, that the body of no deceased person shall be buried in such free ground without the written permission of the mayor. Free ground. Proviso.

Sec. 5. The city clerk shall keep a book in which he shall record the description of all lots, blocks or half blocks sold, together with the price paid therefor and the date of each sale; and all moneys paid for such lots, blocks, or half blocks, shall be paid to said clerk before any deed shall be given therefor, and all such moneys so received shall be immediate- Clerk to keep record of sales and description, and pay over moneys.

ly paid by the clerk to the city treasurer and his receipt taken therefor.

Sexton to be annually appointed.

Sec. 6. The common council shall annually appoint a city sexton, who shall hold his office for one year or until the appointment of his successor.

Powers and duty of sexton.

Sec. 7. It shall be the duty of the city sexton, to take general charge of the cemetery, to keep the walks, grounds and avenues thereof in order and free from obstruction, and take care of trees and fences; under the direction of the mayor he shall cause all bodies which have been or hereafter may be interred without permission in any unsold lot of the city, or in any lot the property of another, without the owner's consent, to be removed to the free ground; he shall keep a copy of the plat of the cemetery upon which all lots sold, and all lots for sale with the prices thereof shall be designated; he shall attend to the burial of the bodies of all deceased persons in said ground when application shall have been made to him for that purpose; he shall keep a record of all interments in a book kept for that purpose, in which shall be entered the name, age and disease, or other cause of death as nearly as may be, place of birth, and precise locality of burial, and at the close of his term of office shall make report of the same to the common council; he shall see all ordinances of the city so far as they relate to said cemetery strictly enforced, and for that purpose is hereby declared a police officer with full power as such to arrest any person violating any such ordinance.

Shall keep plat and record.

When shall be policeman.

Sec. 8. The city sexton is permitted to charge the sum of two dollars for the burial of each person in said cemetery; and said sexton shall receive such other compensation for special services, as the common council may determine. Compensation.

Sec. 9. If the city sexton, or any other person, bury, or attempt to bury, any dead body in any sold lot, or in any lot belonging to another, without due authority for so doing; or if any person shall resist the city sexton in the execution of any duty, or refuse or neglect to obey his lawful directions, or shall injure, deface, or destroy any tree, shrub, stone, stake, post, fence, monument, vault, or other fixture, building or thing of value, or ornament in the cemetery, or trespass on any grave in the cemetery, he or they shall severally be subjected to a fine of not less than ten dollars, nor exceeding five hundred dollars, and in default of the payment thereof may be imprisoned for such time as the justice of the peace by whom such fine is imposed shall determine. Penalty for misconduct or destruction of property.

GEO. H. PAUL, *Mayor.*

Passed March 20, 1858.

H. T. West, *City Clerk.*

ORDINANCE NO. V.

OF STREET SUPERVISORS AND THEIR DUTIES.

Section 1. *Be it ordained by the common council of the city of Kenosha:* Before the first Monday Supervisors to be appointed for each ward.

in May of each year, the city council shall appoint one or more street supervisors, not exceeding one for each ward of said city, whose duty it shall be to enforce the performance of labor, or the payment of moneys in the several wards as provided in section 5, chapter 6, of the city charter; and under the advice of the aldermen of their respective wards, to direct the time, manner, and place in which such labor or money shall be applied, and said supervisors shall give bonds for the faithful discharge of such duties.

Shall make listed polls.

Sec. 2. Each supervisor immediately upon his appointment shall make out and keep a list of the names of all such persons as are subject to highway work in the ward under his charge, and shall give two days notice to all such persons, either personally or by a written or printed notice left at the usual place of abode of any such person, of the time when and the place where he may appear either in person or by a substitute, and perform the labor required; and in case any such person so notified shall fail to appear and to perform said labor, or to pay said supervisor in lieu thereof the sum of two dollars, said supervisor may then, or at any time thereafter, sue and collect such money of said person in accordance with the provisions of the city charter in such case, together with the costs of suit; and in default of the payment of such sum and costs by any such person so sued, such person may be imprisoned in the county jail for a time not less than two days nor more than ten days, in the discretion of the justice.

Shall give notice.

When may sue for and collect.

Sec. 3. Every street supervisor shall render to the common council a report in writing, at the first regular meeting of the council, in each of the months of August and November, containing a statement of the amount of street taxes collected in his ward, and the names of the persons from whom the same was collected in labor and those paid in money, also the manner in which such taxes have been disbursed.— Every such street supervisor shall also at the first regular meeting of the common council in the month of March in each year, render to said common council a report in writing, verified by his affidavit taken before the mayor or some justice of the peace of said city, showing: When shall make reports.

1st. The name of every person in his ward liable to pay street tax or highway tax, and against whom such was charged by him.

2d. The amount of tax collected from such persons stating whether paid in labor, money or otherwise.

3d. The number of days actually employed by the said street supervisor in superintending the expenditure of the taxes on the highways by him collected.

4th. The amount of tax collected and retained by said street supervisor for his services.

5th. The amount of money, if any, accruing from street taxes remaining in the hands of said street supervisor.

Sec. 4. If any moneys shall be remaining in the hands of the said street supervisor, at the time of his making the report prescribed in the preceeding sec- Shall pay over to treasurer surplus moneys.

tion, he shall immediately pay over the same into the city treasury.

Compensation of supervisors.

Sec. 5. Each supervisor shall be allowed such sum for every day actually and necessarily employed by him in the discharge of the duties required of him by this ordinance, as may be determined by the common council

Limit of time for collecting and expending street tax.

Sec. 6. It shall be the duty of the several street supervisors to cause at least two-thirds of the street taxes in their respective wards to be collected and expended, agreeably to the provisions of this ordinance, before the first day of August in each year, and the residue thereof, before the first day of November in each such year.

Provision for removal of supervisors.

Suit to be commenced when money not paid over.

Sec. 7. If any street supervisor shall neglect or refuse properly to perform any of the duties enjoined upon him by this ordinance, the common council, upon satisfactory evidence thereof, may remove such street supervisor from office, and appoint another in his place; and if any such street supervisor shall refuse to pay over any moneys which may be in his hands accruing from street taxes, at the time of his removal from office, or if any street supervisor shall neglect or refuse to pay over any moneys in his hands, at any time when required by the provisions of this ordinance, it shall be the duty of the city treasurer forthwith to sue for the same in the name of the city of Kenosha.

GEO. H. PAUL, *Mayor.*

Passed March 20, 1858.

H. T. West, *City Clerk.*

ORDINANCE NO. VI.

FOR THE REGULATION OF STREETS AND ALLEYS.

Marshal or aldermen may remove obstruction

SECTION 1. *Be it ordained by the common council of the city of Kenosha :* That whenever any person shall encumber or obstruct any street, alley or side-walk in said city, the mayor, city marshal, or any alderman may order the owner, or any person causing such encumbrance or obstruction, to remove the same; or if the owner or person causing such encumbrance or obstruction cannot readily be found, the said mayor, city marshal, or any alderman may cause such obstruction or encumbrance to be removed to some suitable place, to be designated by the mayor, or common council; and the owner of any article so removed, shall forfeit and pay a penalty of two dollars, and in addition shall pay the cost of such removal.

Articles to be advertised and sold.

SEC. 2. Any article or thing of value which may be removed in accordance with the preceding section, may be advertised by the marshal, and sold by him, after thirty days shall have expired from the time of said removal, unless the same shall be sooner claimed, and the penalty and the expense of removal paid by the owner thereof. The said marshal after any such sale, shall pay the proceeds thereof into the city treasury, and furnish the said treasurer with a description of the article sold, and the amount for which the same was sold; and the balance, after the payment of the expenses of such removal and sale, if any, shall be paid by the city treasurer to the person or persons furnishing satisfactory proof of ownership.

Ditches, &c not to be dug without consent

Sec. 3. No person shall dig any hole, drain, or ditch, in any street or alley in this city without first having obtained consent of the mayor, marshal, or an alderman of the city, under a penalty of five dollars for each such offence, and a like penalty for each day any such hole, drain, or ditch shall remain unfilled; and in default of the payment of any such penalty, shall be imprisoned in the county jail five days.

Earth and gravel not to be removed without consent of the mayor.

Sec. 4. If any person shall, without first having obtained the written consent of the mayor or council, dig or carry away, or cause the same to be done, any sod, earth, sand, or gravel, from any street, alley, or public ground in said city, such person shall forfeit and pay a penalty of five dollars for every such offence, and in default of the payment thereof shall be imprisoned five days in the county jail.

Penalty.

Persons prohibited from building in streets and alleys.

Sec. 5. No person shall erect or place any building, in whole or in part, upon any street, alley or upon any public ground in this city, permanently or temporarily, under a penalty of twenty-five dollars for every thirty days, such building shall so remain, after the owner, occupant or agent thereof shall have been notified by the mayor or city marshal to remove the same; and in default of the payment of each such penalty, the offender shall be imprisoned in the county jail twenty-five days.

Penalty.

Sec. 6. No person shall ride or drive any horse, wagon, cart, sled, or other vehicle, over any sidewalk, or plank-walk, unless it be at the crossings of the streets, under a penalty of one dollar for each offence. Not to drive on sidewalks.

GEO. H. PAUL, *Mayor.*

Passed February 20, 1858.

H. T. West, *City Clerk.*

ORDINANCE NO. II.

AN ORDINANCE CONCERNING THE FIRE DEPARTMENT.

Section 1. *Be it ordained by the common council of the city of Kenosha:* The fire department of the the city of Kenosha shall consist of a chief engineer three assistant engineers, one fire warden for each ward in said city, and such other officers, enginemen, hose men, and hook and ladder men as may be appointed by the common council. Fire department, how constituted.

Sec. 2. The chief engineer, and in his absence the assistant engineers, according to rank, shall in all cases of fire have absolute control over all the members of the fire department. Chief engineer, his powers, &c.

Sec. 3. It shall be the duty of the chief engineer on or before the first Monday in November in each year to report to the common council the condition of the engines, hose, hooks and ladders, buckets and oth- Engineer to report condition of apparatus, &c.

fire apparatus, and the buildings in which they are kept; and also to recommed such additions, alterations and improvements to the same as he may deem expedient; and he shall report to the council the names of all persons who shall have been elected members of the different companies.

Division into companies, how made.

Sec. 4. The firemen shall be divided into companies of engine men, hook and ladder men, and hose men, and the common council shall, whenever it may deem necessary, determine the number or men which shall belong to each company.

Companies may adopt constitution

Sec. 5. Each of said companies respectively may adopt such constitution, by-laws and regulations for their government, subordinate to the ordinances of the city, as they may deem best calculated to accomplish the objects hereby contemplated; and each of said companies shall, at such time as it shall determine in each year, choose from among their own number a foreman, a first and second assistant foreman, a clerk and a foreman of the hose company attached to or running with each of the engine companies, and such other officers as they may require in accordance with their respective constitutions or by-laws and in the manner provided therein.

Must be present at fires.

Sec. 6. The different fire companies under the control and direction of their proper officers shall, upon an alarm of fire, repair to the place of the fire with the engines and other fire apparatus under their care, and there work and manage the same under the direction of the chief engineer and his assistants, and in case of their absence, place and work their engines and other fire apparatus in the most effectual manner until the fire shall be extinguished, and shall not remove therefrom but by permission from an engineer, if any shall be present, and on such permission they shall return their engines and fire apparatus, well washed and cleansed, to their respective places of deposit. If any company shall, without permission of an engineer as above, leave any fire with their engine or fire apparatus, the officer in command of such company shall forfeit and pay not less than three nor more than twenty-five dollars for each and every such offence. Penalties for leaving fires.

Sec. 7. The said engines and other fire apparatus shall be kept in such places respectively as the common council shall provide and dessignate, and the several companies having charge of them shall keep the same in the best order for immediate use. Engines, where and how to be kept.

Sec. 8. For the more effectually perfecting the firemen in their duties and preserving the organization of the fire department, and keeping the engines and other apparatus in good order, the said companies shall hold meetings at such times and places as the chief engineer or a majority of the members of said companies may determine. Meetings, when held.

Sec. 9. There shall be a general review of the fire department, engines and other apparatus, by the mayor and aldermen once in each year, on such day and at such place as the chief engineer shall appoint; and at the time and place so appointed, it shall be Annual review, when held.

the duty of all persons belonging to any division of the fire department to appear fully equipped, together with their respective engines and other fire apparatus. Any member of the fire department failing to so appear having received due notice, shall forfeit and pay for the benefit of the company to which he belongs, not less than one nor more than five dollars.

Penalty.

Members of companies, when may be sued.

Sec. 10. Whenever any member of any company of the fire department shall be justly indebted to said company, in pursuance of the constitution, by-laws or regulations of the same, the said constitution, by-laws or regulations having first been submitted to and approved by the common council, it shall be lawful for said company to sue for and receive from such member, on his refusal or neglect to pay, whatever sum may be so due, by action of debt in the name of the city, for the use of said company, before any court having jurisdiction.

Chief engineer may give permit to leave the city.

Sec. 11. The acting chief engineer shall have the power in his discretion to grant permission to any fire company to go with their respective engines and other fire apparatus beyond the limits of the city, to be absent such length of time as he may direct.—Any officer in command of any company who shall suffer or permit the engine or other apparatus in charge of said company to be taken beyond the limits of the city without such permission, shall forfeit and pay for every such offense a penalty of not less than five nor more than twenty-five dollars, besides being liable for all damages.

Duty of fire wardens.

Sec. 12. It shall be the duty of the fire wardens at least twice in each year, one of which times shall be in the month of November, and as as much oftener as they may deem necessary, at proper hours, to visit each store, dwelling, factory, shop, out-house or lot in their respective wards, and examine into the condition of all chimneys, stove pipes, fire places and other matters which in their opinion may be dangerous in causing or producing fires; and such wardens respectively may give directions to the occupant or owner of said buildings, if necessary, for their better security: and in case the owner or occupant shall neglect or refuse, for the space of ten days next thereafter, so to secure or remove the said building, the said wardens shall have the same secured at the expense of the corporation, which sums so expended shall be recovered by the city for the use of the corporation, in an action for the same against either the owner or occupant of said building.

Expense, how may be recovered.

Foreman of each company to report.

Sec. 13. It shall be the duty of the foreman of every fire company, annually at such time as said engineer may designate, to make to the chief engineer a complete return of the name of each member of his company, under the penalty of five dollars.

Penalty.

What deemed necessary to make stove secure

Sec. 14. All persons using a stove, shall have a piece of sheet iron, tin, zinc or other material, as security against fire, placed underneath such stove, and shall have the partition through which any stove pipe shall pass secured from fire by earthen, stone or such other funnels as the wardens may in each case direct, under a penalty of five dollars for each offence against the provisions of this section.

Firemen exempt from poll tax.

Sec. 15. The firemen of this city shall be exempt from poll tax.

Powers of chief engineer, mayor, &c., at fires.

Sec. 16. It shall be lawful for the chief engineer, his assistants, the mayor and any member of the common council, to order any able bodied male person present at any fire, when necessary, to help the firemen work their engines, ladders, hooks, or other fire apparatus: and if any person being so ordered shall neglect or refuse to obey any such order, he shall, upon conviction thereof, be fined ten dollars, to be sued for and recovered as other penalties are under the city ordinances, and when so recovered shall be paid to the treasurer of the fire department of the city of Kenosha for the benefit of said department, and in default of the payment of any such fine the person liable to pay the same shall be imprisoned in the county jail for the term of five days.

GEO. H. PAUL, *Mayor.*

Passed March 20, 1858.

H. T. WEST, *City Clerk.*

ORDINANCE NO. VIII.

FOR THE SECURITY OF PERSONS AND PROPERTY.

Fire arms, how may be used.

SECTION 1. *Be it ordained by the common council of the city of Kenosha:* That no person shall fire or discharge any cannon, rifle, gun, pistol, or fire arms of any description, or fire, explode, or set off any squib, cracker, or other thing containing powder or other combustible or explosive material in any street, alley, or public ground within this city south of a line running through Lemon street from the lake to the west line of the corporation, and east of West Main street, without the permission of the common council, or the written permission of the mayor, which permission shall limit the time of such firing, and shall be subject to be revoked by the mayor or common council at any time after it has been granted.— Any person who shall violate this section shall for each offence forfeit and pay a penalty of three dollars; and in default of the payment of such penalty, shall be imprisoned in the county jail two days, and one half of each fine imposed in such case when collected shall be paid to the person who shall make the complaint before any justice of the peace.

Penalty.

Penalty for fast driving.

SEC. 2. Every person who shall ride or drive any horse, in any street or alley within the limits of this city south of Lemon street, and east of West Main street, faster than a moderate trot, or at any greater speed than six miles an hour, shall forfeit and pay a fine of five dollars ; and in default of the payment of of such penalty shall be imprisoned in the county jail five days.

Fast driving on bridges prohibited.

Sec. 3. That all riding or driving over Main and Grand street bridges in this city, faster than a walk, is hereby expressly prohibited; and any person who may be found violating the provisions of this ordinance shall be subject to a fine of five dollars; and in default of the payment of said fine, to imprisonment in the county jail two days. Said fine, when collected, shall be paid to the person or persons who shall make complaint to any justice of the peace of this city.

Penalty.

Limit of speed of locomotives, &c.

Sec. 4. That a greater speed of traveling than six miles per hour, or at that rate, by any locomotive, railroad car, or other vehicle, upon any railroad track running through or into the city of Kenosha is hereby prohibited, and for every violation of this section, the offending party shall be subject to a fine of twenty-five dollars, one half of which fine when collected shall be paid to the party entering complaint before any justice of the peace of this city.

Penalty.

Limit of quantity of gunpowder which may be kept.

Sec. 5. No person shall be allowed to keep any gunpowder in any occupied building within the limits of this city without permission of the council;—and no person shall keep in any such building a greater quantity than ten pounds; which shall be kept in a close tin canister or canisters. Every person violating any provisions of this section, shall, upon conviction thereof, be fined twenty dollars, which it shall be lawful for the treasurer of the fire department of this city to sue for in the name of the city of Kenosha; and such fines when collected shall be paid to the said treasurer for the use of the fire department; and in default of such payment, the person or persons convicted shall be imprisoned in the county jail of this county for the term of ten days. Penalty.

Sec. 6. No person or persons shall stack any hay, straw or other combustible substance within fifty feet of any store, dwelling house or shop within the limits of the city of Kenosha, without first obtaining the written permission of the mayor, and the alderman of the ward in which the same may be located, under a penalty of twenty-five dollars for each offence, and a like penalty for every ten days the same may remain after notice in writing to remove the same from the mayor, any alderman or fire warden of said city. Limits of stacking hay.

GEO. H. PAUL, *Mayor.*

Passed March 20, 1858.

H. T. WEST, *City Clerk.*

ORDINANCE NO. IX.

AN ORDINANCE FOR THE PROTECTION OF PUBLIC GROUNDS.

Penalty for mutilation, destruction, or injury.

Section 1. *Be it ordained by the common council of the city of Kenosha:* If any person except by authority of the mayor and committee on public grounds, shall destroy, mutilate, remove, cut, break or injure any tree, shrub, plant, or any ornament or ornaments whatever, on any public grounds, within any cemetery, or upon any street, or within any public square, or parks of this city, or shall in any way injure the fences or gates around any such inclosure, such person so offending shall be punished by a fine not less than three nor more than twenty-five dollars, or by imprisonment in the county jail not less than five nor more than thirty days, in the discretion of the justice before whom conviction may be had.

Penalty for letting animals upon parks, &c.

Sec. 2. Whoever shall turn into any inclosed public square or park of this city, any horse, cow, swine or other animal, by reason of which any damage is liable to accrue, or shall accrue to any tree, shrub, plant, or any ornament or fixtures whatever, placed or being within any such enclosure, the person so offending shall be punished by fine, not less than three nor more than twenty-five dollars, or by imprisonment in the county jail not less than five nor more than thirty days, in the discretion of the justice before whom any conviction under this ordinance may be had.

GEO. H. PAUL, *Mayor*,

Passed February 20, 1858.

H. T. West, City Clerk.

ORDINANCE NO. X.

AN ORDINANCE CONCERNING THE CONTRACTING OF DEBTS AND THE CHARGE OF THE PUBLIC PROPERTY.

When city not liable for debts contracted by officers, &c.

Section 1. *Be it ordained by the common council of the city of Kenosha:* No officer or employee of the city shall have power to contract any debt or incur any expenditure except by order or resolution of the common council, and the city shall not be held liable for the payment of any debt so contracted or expense so incurred.

Contracts to be in writing and filed.

Sec. 2. Every contract or agreement made or entered into by or on behalf of the city shall be in writing and in duplicate, and for a sum certain for the performance of the entire work; one copy of which contract shall in each case be filed with the city clerk.

Harbor tools, &c. who to have charge.

Sec. 3. The chairman of the harbor committee shall have direct charge of all property of the city owned or purchased for the work upon the harbor; the chairman of the committee on roads and bridges shall have direct charge of all property owned or purchased for the purpose of street work or work upon bridges; and all other property belonging to the

Road tools, &c., materials, who to have charge

Mayor to have custody of remainder.

city not hereinbefore mentioned, shall be in charge of the mayor. A list of such property shall in each case be filed by each of said officers with the city clerk at the commencement of his term of service, and a receipt given therefor.

Penalty for self-appropriation by officers.

Sec. 4. Any alderman or other officer of the city of Kenosha who shall appropriate to his own use and for his own private benefit any money, goods, lumber, iron, tools, or materials, or property of any sort whatever, without the explicit consent of the common council; or if any alderman or other officer of the city shall refuse to account for any property in his charge, either when requested to so by the council, or at the expiration of his term of office, he shall pay to the city of Kenosha the full value of said property, and in addition shall pay a fine of not less than twenty-five dollars nor more than one hundred dollars for each such offence.

Officers, &c. to prosecute against ordinance.

Sec. 5. It is hereby made the duty of any officer of the city, or other person who shall have knowledge of any offence mentioned in the preceding section, to complain of and prosecute the offender before any justice of the peace of this city; and if any such offence shall be committed by any alderman of the city, he shall be liable to the penalties prescribed in the preceding section, and also be forthwith expelled from the council.

GEO. H. PAUL, *Mayor*.

Passed March 24, 1858.

H. T. West, *City Clerk*.

ORDINANCE NO. XI.

FOR THE PRESERVLTION OF THE PUBLIC HEALTH.

Board of health, how constituted.

SECTION 1. *Be it ordained by the common council of the city of Kenosha:* The mayor, city physician, and such other persons not exceeding three, or as the common council may deem it necessary to appoint, shall constitue a board of health, whose duty it shall be to inquire and examine into all nuisances, sources of filth, and causes of disease, which they may deem dangerous to the health and lives of the inhabitants of said city; and the said board of health shall have power to order the removal of all such nuisances, source of filth, and causes of disease.

Power of board to remove nuisances.

Sec. 2. The board of health, or any person acting under their directions, shall have power, in the day time to enter into any building, cellar, yard, inclosure, or upon any lot of ground, in said city, and examine as to any nuisance, or cause of disease, and may direct the cleansing of any such building, cellar yard, inclosure or lot, and the removal of all nuisances in and about such premises. Every person who shall neglect or refuse to comply with any order or direction of the said board of health as aforesaid, shall forfeit and pay a fine of five dollars for every twenty-four hours such order or direction shall not be complied with; and in default of the payment of any such fine, shall be imprisoned in the county jail five days.

Penalty.

Duty of board.

Sec. 3. Whenever any putrid or unsound beef, pork fish, hides, or skins of any kind, or any other putrid or unsound substance shall be found in any part of said city, it shall be the duty of the board of health to cause the same to be destroyed, removed or disposed of in such manner as the good of the public health may require.

Penalty for conducting any offensive matter into any street, alley, or lot.

Sec. 4. If any person shall throw, place or conduct, or suffer any one under his control, or in his employ, to throw, place or conduct into any street, alley, public ground, or lot, any filth, offal, animal or vegetable matter, or any offensive matter whatever or anything likely to become offensive matter; or shall allow any such filth, offal, or other offensive matter, to remain in his stable, out-house, yard, or any inclosure, on his premises or the premises by him occupied, in such manner as to be offensive to the neighborhood of such premises, every such person shall be fined in the sum of three dollars, and in default of the payment thereof shall be imprisoned in the county jail three days.

Provision for cleaning of gutters, ditches, &c.

Sec. 5. Whenever any gutter, ditch, or drain, in front of any store, shop, or dwelling, barn, or any other building whatever, or on the lot to which any such building is attatched or belongs, shall become filled with stagnant water, or obstructed by any filth offal, or putrid substance of any kind, it shall be the duty of any member of the board of health, any alderman, or the city marshal, to order the owner, occupant, or agent of such premises, to remove or abate such nuisance, and if any such owner, occupant or agent of such premises, shall neglect or refuse to remove or abate such nuisance, after twenty-four hours notice from any one of the aforesaid officers, he shall forfeit and pay a fine of ten dollars.

Sec. 6. If any person in said city, not being a resident thereof, shall be infected with any contagious disease, the board of health may order such person to be removed to some proper place, not more than three miles beyond the limits of the said city, provided such removal can be effected without danger to the health of such person,

Diseased non-residents, how may be removed.

Sec 7. Whenever any expense shall be incurred in the removal or abatement of any nuisances or causes of disease, according to the provisions of this ordinance, shall be recovered, together with all costs of suit, from the persons in each case liable to remove or abate the same according to the provisions of this ordinance.

Expense of abating nuisances, to be paid by the person liable.

GEO. H. PAUL, *Mayor.*

Passed February 20, 1858.

H. T. WEST, *City Clerk.*

ORDINANCE NO. XII.

OF OFENCES AGAINST PUBLIC ORDER AND MORALS.

Penalty for disturb-ances.

SECTION 1. *Be it ordained by the common council of the city of Kenosha:* That whenever any person or persons shall make, aid, countenance, or assist in making any improper noise or disturbance in the streets, or elsewhere, within the limits of said city; or whenever any persons shall collect in crowds creating public disorder, or for unlawful purposes to the annoyance or disturbance of citizens or travelers, or of any public meeting lawfully and peacefully assembled, every such person so offending shall forfeit for each such offence a penalty not exceeding ten dollars, and in default of the payment thereof, shall be imprisoned in the county jail ten days.

Penalty for indecent exposure.

Sec. 2. Any person found in a state of intoxication in any public or exposed place, or any person guilt of any act of public indecency, lewdness, or immodest public exposure, or of letting any stud horse to any mare, or indecently exhibiting such horse in any exposed or public place, within the limits of said city, shall for each or either offence forfeit and pay a fine not exceeding fifteen dollars; or in default of the payment thereof shall be imprisoned in the county jail fifteen days.

Sec. 3. If any person shall be guilty of keeping

or maintaining, or shall be an inmate of, or in any way contribute to the support of any disorderly house or house of ill-fame, or place for the practice of fornication, or shall knowingly and wilfully own or be interested as landlord or proprietor of any such house every such person shall on conviction forfeit and pay a fine of not exceeding fifty dollars, and a further fine of twenty-five dollars for every twenty-four hours such house shall be continued after the first conviction, or after any such person shall be ordered by any member of the common council, the city marshal or any constable of the city, to suppress, restrain or discontinue the same; and in case of non-payment of any fine imposed by the provisions of this section, the offender shall be imprisoned in the county jail not exceeding forty days.

Penalty for keeping disorderly houses.

Who may order suppression.

Sec. 4. No person shall have, keep, or permit to be used in any building or place within the city, used, occupied, or controlled by such person, any gaming table, playing cards, or any instrument, device or thing used for gambling whereon or with which money shall in any manner be played for, under a penalty of not exceeding twenty dollars: and any person on whom such penalty may be imposed shall in default of the payment thereof, be imprisoned in the county jail twenty days.

Penalty against gambling devices.

Sec. 5. The mayor or any alderman, the city marshal, or any constable of the city, may seize or direct to be seized any instrument, device or thing to be used by, on, or with which money may be lost or

Who may seize and destroy gambling instruments

won, and all such instruments, devices or things, may be demolished or destroyed under the direction of the mayor.

When gaming houses &c. may be forcibly entered, &c.

Sec. 6. If the owner or keeper of, or any person within any gambling house, room, disorderly house, or house of ill-fame within the city, shall refuse to permit the mayor, or any alderman, the city marshal or any constable of said city, to enter the same, it shall be lawful for the mayor or any alderman to enter, or cause to be entered, by force, by breaking the doors or otherwise, and arrest with or without process all suspicious persons found therein.

Not to swim in city limits.

Sec. 7. No person shall, between the hours of sunrise and sunset, swim or bathe in the waters of Pike Creek, or Lake Michigan within the limits of this city. Every person violating this section, shall forfeit and pay for each offence, a fine of two dollars and in default of the payment of such fine, shall be imprisoned in the county jail one day.

V. HUGHES, *Mayor*.

Passed May 19, 1856.

H. T. WEST, *City Clerk*.

ORDINANCE NO. XIII.

AN ORDINANCE RESTRAINING AND REGULATING THE SALE OF SPIRITUOUS LIQUORS.

Licenses, when and how may be granted.

Section 1. *Be it ordained by the common council of the city of Kenosha:* License to sell spirituous, vinous, or fermented liquors, as well as transfers of such licenses, may be granted at any time to any person or persons applying for the same at the discretion of the common council, upon such persons executing a bond with at least two sureties to be approved by the council in the penal sum of ($300) three hundred dollars, conditioned that the party so licensed shall faithfully observe and keep all ordinances of the city now in force, or which shall be passed during the period of such license for the regulation and control of the traffic in said liquors: all such licenses and transfers to be signed by the mayor and countersigned by the clerk: and to be delivered to the applicant on the production of a certificate from the city treasurer that the full amount charged for such license has been paid. *Provided,* That all licenses hereafter granted shall terminate on the first Monday in May of each year.

Proviso.

When license may be revoked.

Sec. 2. Any license or transfer of license so granted, may be revoked by the common council whenever it shall satisfactorily appear that the party so licensed shall have violated any provision of any ordinance of the common council relating to spirituous liquors, or any condition of the bond aforesaid; and all persons licensed under this or any other ordinance or rule of said city relating to the sale of said liquors, shall immediately cause to be and remain posted upon some conspicuous part of the room, or bar kept or used for such purpose, his her, or their license. Any person so licensed who shall not cause such license to be and remain posted as aforesaid, or who not being so licensed shall cause or permit any paper or thing purporting to be a license, to be and remain posted as aforesaid, shall on conviction be fined not less than five nor more than twenty dollars.

License to be posted in bar, &c.

Penalty.

Clerk to make out papers.

Sec. 3. The necessary bonds, licenses, and transfers of the same, shall be made by the city clerk, who shall be entitled to demand and receive from the applicant in full for all services connected with each license the sum of one dollar.

Clerk to keep register of date, &c.

Sec. 4. The clerk shall keep a license register in which shall be entered the names of all persons now or hereafter to be licensed; the place of business; the date of the license; and the time when the same will expire in each case, together with the sums received therefor; and shall make a quarterly report of the same to the council. All licenses shall be dated of the day when the same were severally granted: and no person shall be deemed to be duly licensed to whom a license has not been actually issued, or transferred and posted as aforesaid.

Public vending of liquors on Sunday by

Sec. 5. All persons to whom license to sell spirituous, vinuous, or fermented liquors has heretofore been, or to whom such license shall hereafter be granted, are hereby prohibited from opening his, her, or their bar, or place for the sale of such liquors, with intent to sell, give away or in any manner deal in, and from selling, giving away or in any manner dealing in, by himself, servant, or any other person, any spirituous, vinous, or mixed, fermented or intoxicating liquors on the first day of the week called Sunday; and from gaming with or without betting by means of cards, dominoes, or any other device on that day; and every such person or persons having such license, shall if found guilty of violating any of the provisions of this section, forfeit his, her, or their said license, and be subject to a fine of ten dollars, and in default of the payment of such fine shall be imprisoned in the county jail for a period not exceeding thirty days nor less than ten days. License prohibited. Gaming also prohibited. Penalty.

Sec. 6. Any person who shall hereafter have or keep any tavern, grocery, ordinary, victualling or other house or place within the city for the selling, giving away, or in any manner dealing in any vinous, spirituous, ardent, intoxicating, or fermented liquors, or who by himself, his agent or servant, shall sell, give away, or in any manner deal in any such liquors without a license in pursuance of the provisions of this ordinance, shall upon conviction thereof be subject to a fine of not less than ten dollars nor more than one hundred dollars. *Provided*, that druggists, or persons whose chief business is to sell drugs and medicines, shall not be subject to the Penalty for selling without license. Proviso.

provisions of this ordinance in selling liquors for purposes purely medicinal, mechanical, or sacramental; and in all cases of conviction under this section, the court or magistrate shall have power, in its discretion, to sentence the offender to the county jail for a period not exceeding sixty days.

Repealing clause. Sec. 7. All ordinances, rules, and regulations of of the common council conflicting with the provisions of this ordinance are hereby repealed.

GEO. H. PAUL, *Mayor.*

Passed May 17, 1858.

H. T. West, *City Clerk.*

ORDINANCE NO. XIV.

TO RESTRAIN THE RUNNING AT LARGE OF CERTAIN ANIMALS.

Pound master and pound. Section 1. *Be it ordained by the common council of the city of Kenosha:* That there may be appointed in each year by the said common council a pound master for said city, who shall hold his office during the pleasure of the said council and until his successor is appointed; the said common council may also order the construction of a city pound, suitable for impounding animals, as provided in this ordinance.

Sec. 2. No horse shall be permitted to run at large within the limits of the said city; or in any enclosed public square or park thereof, and if any horse shall be found so running at large, such horse may be impounded in the pound of said city, and may be sold at public auction by the pound master thereof, at any time after the expiration of ten days from the time such horse shall have been impounded, on giving five days public notice of such sale, to be posted in three public places in said city, specifying the time and place of sale and a description of the property to be sold.

Horses not to run at large.

Sec. 3. No swine or geese shall be permitted to run at large within the limits of this city or in any enclosed public square or park thereof, nor shall any cattle be permitted to run at large in any enclosed public square or park of said city at any time; and if found so running at large, each and every such animal may be impounded in the pound of said city and may be sold at public auction at any time after such animal shall have been impounded, on giving not less than three days notice of such sale, posted up in three public places in said city, specifying the time and place of such sale.

Swine and geese not to run large.

Sec. 4. From the first day of November until the first day of March, no ox, steer, cow, heifer or bull shall be permitted to run at large in the first or fourth wards of the city of Kenosha, within the following prescribed limits, to wit: All that portion of said wards lying between the south line of south street

When cattle not to run at large in city limits.

and the south line of the creek, and east of the west side of church street, and if found so running at large each and every animal may be impounded in the pound of said city, and may be sold at public auction after such animal may have been impounded, on giving not less than ten days notice of such sale, said notice to be posted in not less than three public places in said city specifying the time and place of such sale.

Cows not to run at large at night. Sec. 5. No cow shall be permitted to run at large within the limits of the city of Kenosha, during the night time from 8 o'clock P. M., to 5 o'clock A. M., and if found so running at large, each and every such cow may be impounded in the pound of said city, and may be sold at public auction at any time after such cow or cows shall have been impounded, on giving not less than six days notice of said sale, posted up in three public places in said city specifying the time and place of such sale.

Compensation of pound master. Sec. 6. Every pound keeper shall be entitled for receiving into the pound of said city a compensation as follows: For every horse received into said pound twenty-five cents, and fifty cents for every twenty four hours such horse shall be kept therein. For every swine received into said pound, twenty-five cents ; for every goose twelve and a half cents, and for every twenty-four hours each such swine chall be kept therein, twenty-five cents, and twelve and a half cents for every goose. For giving notice of sale, as provided in sections two, three, four and five of this ordinance, thirty-seven and a half cents; for selling every horse, one dollar; for selling swine, twenty-five cents, each; for selling geese, twelve and a half cents each; for selling each animal mentioned in section four, fifty cents each.

Disposition of moneys received by pound master.

Sec. 7. The money reoeived by any pound keeper after deducting the costs and charges allowed by the provisions of this ordinance, shall be paid to the city treasurer, and the same shall be delivered to the owner of the animal or animals, from the sale of which such money shall have accrued, if such owner shall appear within two years from the time of said sale and render satisfactory proof to the mayor, of title to said animal or animals; and in case no such owner shall appear, claim, and give satisfactory proof as above provided, then such money shall be forfeited to, and become the property of said city.

Animals to be delivered to owners upon payment of charges and fees.

Sec. 8. The owner of any animal mentioned in this ordinance that shall have been impounded, may claim such animal to be released therefrom on payment to the pound master the charges and fees that shall have accrued agreeably to the provisions of this ordinance, at any time before the sale of any such animal, on giving satisfactory proof of title thereto.

Description of animals to be recorded.

Sec. 9. It shall be the duty of the pound master on receiving any animal, to enter a description thereof in a book to be kept for that purpose by him, together with the date of such entry, and he shall also enter in such book every sale made by him, the amount received therefrom, and the amount of his fees and charges thereon; and if the animal or money shall be claimed, an entry thereof shall be made and if the animal or money shall be delivered to the claimant, his receipt therefor shall be taken in such book.

Animals may be taken up by any person.

Sec. 10. Any person may take up and deliver to the pound keeper to be impounded, or cause the same to be done, any animal running at large, contrary to the provisions of this ordinance; and if any pound keeper appointed as aforesaid shall neglect or refuse to take up, distrain, or impound any animals known by him to be running at large, contrary to the provisions of this ordinance, he shall forfeit and pay a fine of ten dollars for each and every such refusal or neglect.

Penalty for breaking open pound

Sec. 11. If any person or persons shall break open, or in any way, directly or indirectly, aid or assist in breaking open the pound of said city, every such person shall forfeit and pay a penalty of twenty dollars, and in default of the payment of such penalty shall be imprisoned in the county jail ten days.

Penalty for obstructing the execution of this ordinance.

Sec. 12. Every person who shall hinder, delay, or obstruct any person or persons, engaged in driving to the pound of said city any animal or animals mentioned in this ordinance, shall forfeit and pay a fine for every such hindrance, delay, or obstruction, of five dollars, and in case of the non-payment of such fine shall be imprisoned in the county jail three days.

Sec. 13. It shall be the duty of the pound keeper of said city to provide necessary sustenance for all animals impounded in the said city pound, without further charge than is prescribed or allowed by section four of this ordinance. Impounded animals to be provided with sustenance.

GEO. H. PAUL, *Mayor.*

Passed March 20, 1858.

H. T. WEST, *City Clerk.*

ORDINANCE NO. XV.

RELATING TO THE EXHIBITION OF SHOWS, SHOWMEN, AND OTHER PERFORMANCES.

Section 1. *Be it ordained by the common council of the city of Kenosha:* That it shall not be lawful for any person or persons to exhibit for gain, within this city, any animal or animals, wax or other figures, or paintings, feats of circus riding, rope or wire dancing, sleight of hand, or any theatrical or musical entertainment, without first having obtained a license therefor; and if any person shall offend against the provisions of this section, he shall pay for each offence a sum not less than fifteen dollars nor more than fifty dollars, and costs of prosecution, to be re- License for exhibitions.

covered on complaint before any court having competent jurisdiction; and in default of the payment of such fine and costs, shall be imprisoned in the jail of Kenosha county not less than one day nor more than thirty days, at the discretion of the court or justice rendering judgment.

Penalty.

Who to grant licenses.

Sec. 2. It shall be the duty of the mayor to grant the licenses herein provided for, if, in his opinion, the exhibition will not injuriously affect the morals of the people, or offend against the rules of decency and good order; and he shall, in his discretion, fix the sum to be paid for licenses in all cases not herein provided.

Sums fixed for licenses.

Sec. 3. The following shall be the rates of license for the exhibitions or shows specified: For a circus the sum of twenty dollars for every day's performance; for a menagerie, the sum of fifteen dollars for every day's exhibition; for a theatre, the sum of three dollars for each and every time of performance or the sum of twelve dollars for one week of six successive days; and for sleight of hand or jugglery performances, the sum of five dollars for each and every time of performance.

How license to issue.

Sec. 4. No license shall be issued until the person applying for the same shall present the marshal's receipt for the amount fixed by ordinanee or by the mayor, and the clerk shall preserve said receipt and make an entry thereof.

What license shall specify.

Sec. 5. Every license granted in pursuance of this ordinance shall specify the time, of its duration, and shall be of no vali dity after the expiration of such time, and no such license shall be assignable for the benefit of any other person.

Sec. 6. It shall be lawful for residents of this city to give concerts or musical entertainments without charge. Who may give free entertainments.

GEO. H. PAUL, *Mayor.*

Passed March 24, 1858.

H. T. WEST, *City Clerk.*

ORDINANCE NO. XVI.

TO PREVENT THE KILLING OF BIRDS.

Section 1. *Be it ordained by the common council of the city of Kenosha:* That the killing of birds by firearms, bow and arrows, or in any other manner, within the city of Kenosha, is hereby prohibited: Every person who shall hereafter kill or wound, or attempt to kill or wound, by fire-arms, bow and arrow, pelting with stones, or otherwise, any bird within the city limits, (such bird so killed or attempted to be killed or wounded, not being the property of the person so offending,) shall forfeit and pay to the city, for every bird so killed or wounded, and for ev- Killing of birds prohibited.

ery such attempt to kill or wound, not less than one nor more than ten dollars.

Penalty for disregard of prohibition. Sec. 2. Every person who shall enter upon any private inclosure, or public ground belonging to the city, for the purpose of doing any act prohibited in the preceding section, and every person who shall shoot an arrow, throw a stone, club, or other missile at any bird within any private grounds, or public parks, squares or grounds, shall forfeit and pay to the city not less than three nor more than ten dollars for each offence.

Penalty for second offence. Sec. 3. Every person who shall be convicted a second time of any offence or penalty hereinbefore mentioned, may, in the discretion of the mayor, be sentenced to the county jail for not less than one nor more than five days.

GEO. H. PAUL, *Mayor.*

Passed May 18, 1857.

H. T. WEST, *City Clerk.*

ORDINANCE NO. XVII.

AN ORDINANCE IN RELATION TO DOGS.

SECTION 1. *Be it ordained by the common council of the city of Kenosha:* That no dog, bitch or whelp shall be allowed or permitted to run at large within the limits of said city, between the first days of June and October of each and every year; and every owner or keeper of any dog, bitch or whelp, who shall permit the same to run or be at large contrary to the provisions of this section, shall pay a penalty of five dollars for each offence; and the informer thereof shall be entitled to one-half of said penalty when collected; *Provided*, That nothing in this ordinance shall authorize the destruction of any dog, bitch or whelp found running at large, if such dog, bitch or whelp shall be securely muzzled with a wire muzzle, to be fastened on with a leather strap or chain; nor shall a suit be commenced against the owner of any such dog found running at large securely muzzled as aforesaid.

Dogs not to run at large at certain seasons.

Penalty.

Dogs muzzled.

SEC. 2. It shall and may be lawful for the mayor of the city of Kenosha to publish his proclamation forbidding the running at large of any dog, bitch or whelp within the limits of said city at any period of the year, whenever in his opinion the public safety is in danger, or that there are mad or rabid dogs within or near said city, unless such dog, bitch or whelp

Mayor may prohibit running at large of dogs at any time.

is securely muzzled, as proviced in this ordinance; and the mayor is hereby authorized and empowered to employ as many persons and at such pay as he may think proper to carry into effect the provisions of this section. It shall and may be lawful for the city marshal, and for such other person or persons as may be authorized by the mayor to kill and destroy or cause to be killed or destroyed, any dog, bitch or whelp which may be found running at large contrary to the provisions herein contained. And it is hereby made the duty of the marshal and the entire police force of the city, upon notice from the mayor, to proceed forthwith to destroy all dogs found so running at large. And any person who shall molest, interrupt, hinder or prevent the city marshal, or any person authorized by the mayor as aforesaid, or either of them, in the discharge of the duty herein prescribed, shall forfeit and pay a penalty of twenty-five dollars for each offence.

Duty of marshal.

Penalty of obstructing officers.

GEO. H. PAUL, *Mayor*,

Passed March 20, 1858.

H. T. West, City Clerk.

ORDINANCE NO. XVIII.

TO REGULATE THE SALE OF HAY AND WOOD.

SECTION 1. *Be it ordained by the common council of the city of Kenosha:* Market square, in the first ward of the city of Kenosha is hereby declared to be and made a public stand for the sale of hay and wood. Market bounds defined.

SEC. 2. No person shall be allowed to expose for sale any hay or wood, or load of hay or wood except in the place designated in the first section of this ordinance. Penalty for using other streets, &c.

SEC. 3. No person shall offer for sale within the limits of the city of Kenosha any hay loaded upon wagon, sled or vehicle without first having obtained a written ticket or certificate of the weight or quantity of hay upon such wagon, sled or other vehicle from the owner or attendant of some established and sealed hay scale within the city limits aforesaid which ticket shall be signed by the owner or attendant of such scale. Weight of hay how to be certified.

SEC. 4. Any person offering hay for sale shall exhibit his ticket of the weight of the same to the purchaser thereof before being entitled to receive pay therefor, under the penalty hereinafter provided. Vender to exhibit his certificate.

SEC. 5. All fire wood offered for sale within the limits of the city of Kenosha loaded upon any wagon Wood how measured and certified.

sled or vehicle shall be first inspected and measured by an inspector to be appointed as hereinafter provided, and such inspector shall give to the owner thereof a written ticket with his signature attached, of the quantity of wood contained in said load.

Penalty for violation of ordinance.

Sec. 6. Any person or persons who shall offer for sale any wood or hay contrary to the provisions of the preceding sections of this ordinance shall forfeit and pay for each and every offence the sum of one dollar, together with the cost of prosecution.

Compensation of weigher and inspector.

Sec. 7. The attendant upon hay scales shall be entitled to receive for weighing each load of hay, fifteen cents, and for weighing wagons, ten cents, and the inspector of wood, five cents for each load of wood, to be paid by the person to whom the ticket for such weight or measurement shall be delivered.

Wood inspector, who may appoint.

Sec. 8. The common council, at the present session of this board, and each year thereafter, shall elect by ballot one inspector of wood, whose office shall expire on the first Tuesday in April, and said inspector before entering upon the duties of his office shall take and subscribe an oath of office, and file the same with the city clerk, and said inspector shall be ex-officio a special policeman, and receive compensation for such special services only as he may perform in legal prosecutions.

May appoint a deputy.

Sec. 9. The inspector of wood may appoint a deputy in any ward in the city in which such inspector does not reside, which appointment shall be subject to confirmation or rejection.

Sec. 10. It is hereby made the duty of the inspector for the sale of wood in this city to enforce the provisions of this ordinance, and to make complaint for any violation of the provisions thereof. Duty of inspector to enforce ordinance

Sec. 11. In case of the non-payment of any of the fines of this ordinance, the offender shall be imprisoned one day for each dollar of fine. Penalty for non-payment of fines.

GEO. H. PAUL, *Mayor.*

Passed January 4, 1858.

H. T. West, *City Clerk.*

ORDINANCE NO. XIX.

TO REGULATE AND RESTRAIN RUNNERS OR SOLICITORS.

Section 1. *Be it ordained by the common council of the city of Kenosha:* That the mayor of the city of Kenosha is hereby authorized and empowered to license such and so many persons as he may deem proper, to act as runners or solicitors for passengers for boats, railroads, public houses, or other establishments, within the limits of the city of Kenosha:— *Provided,* That every person upon being so licensed shall execute to the treasurer of the city of Kenosha a bond with one or more sureties to be approved by the mayor, in the penal sum of one hundred dollars, conditioned to observe the provisions of this ordi- Mayor may license, &c. Proviso.

nance. All licenses granted in pursuance hereof, shall be subject at all times to be revoked by the city council, and shall expire on the first Tuesday of April of each year.

Penalty for misconduct of runners.

Sec. 2. Any person while engaged in the business of runner or solicitor as mentioned in the preceding section, who shall be guilty of using any indecent or profane language, or be guilty of any loud or boisterous talking, or disorderly conduct, or shall obstruct any sidewalk or passage way, or shall harass, vex or disturb strangers or citizens, or use any deceit, imposition or false representation as to any public house, private house, or other locality whatever in said city, shall pay a fine not less than five nor more than twenty dollars.

To wear badge.

Sec. 3. Every runner or solicitor licensed in pursuance of this ordinance, shall, when engaged in the business of running or soliciting for passengers, wear conspicuously on the front of his hat or cap, such badge as shall be designated by the mayor. Any person who shall act as runner or solicitor, as provided in this ordinance, without having a license as such, shall be liable to pay for every offence the sum of five dollars.

Penalty.

GEO. H. PAUL, *Mayor.*

Passed November 6, 1857.

H. T. West, City Clerk.

ORDINANCE NO. XX.

REGULATING THE NUMBERING OF MAIN STREET.

What part of city to be numbered.

Section 1. *Be it ordained by the common council of the city of Kenosha:* That all those portions of Main street between the bridge and South street, shall be numbered as hereinafter provided, commencing at the east side of said street, on lot No. 9, block No. 14

How street shall be numbered.

Sec. 2. The said street shall be numbered progressively, and extending from side to side of said street so that the odd numbers shall be on one side, and the even numbers on the other side of said street.

Sec. 3. And it shall be so numbered that there shall be a number for every twenty-two feet of land fronting upon said street, except where the lots fronting upon said street are 17 feet, or between 17 and 50 feet; in which places the numbering shall be so modified as to give one number to each lot of from 17 to 25 feet, and two numbers to each lot of from 38 to 50 feet or as near as conveniently may be.

Further Provisions.

Sec. 4. The several buildings that are now or hereafter shall be erected on either side of Main street, between the bridge and South street, shall be numbered by the owner or owners, occupant or occupants thereof in the manner following, viz: commencing on the north-west side of Old Main street, at its junction with the river, as number one; thence alternately, from side to side, as aforesaid, extending south to South street.

Size of figures. Sec. 5. The figures of every number shall not be of less dimensions than three inches in length, each figure, and shall be legible and placed in a conspicuous place, on the side or above the front door, in every such building.

Penalties. Sec. 6. Any person or persons, being the owner or owners of any building or buildings, now erected, and being upon and fronting on said street, who shall neglect or refuse to number his or their building or buildings, in conformity with the provisions of this ordinance, shall forfeit a penalty of two dollars, and a further penalty of two dollars for every thirty days the same may be neglected thereafter; and any person or persons who shall hereafter erect any building or buildings on said street, shall within thirty days after the same shall be erected, cause the same to be numbered as aforesaid; and in case of neglecting or refusing so to do, said person or persons shall forfeit and pay to the city the sum of two dollars, and a further penalty of two dollars for every thirty days the same may be neglected thereafter: *Provided*, That no person shall be subject to a penalty under this article, or any order of the common council in conformity thereto, until they shall have had notice

Proviso.

thereof from a street commissioner, or other officer of the city, and have been informed of their appropriate number.

GEO. H. PAUL, *Mayor.*

Passed March 20, 1858.

H. T. WEST, *City Clerk.*

ORDINANCE NO. XXI.

Section 1. *Be it ordained by the common council of the city of Kenosha:* That from and after this date the name of Kenosha street be and the same is hereby changed to Park Avenue, and that hereafter the said street be known and designated as Park Avenue.

Name of Kenosha street changed to Park avenue.

GEO. H. PAUL, *Mayor.*

Passed May 24, 1857.

C. B. LEWIS, *City Clerk.*

ORDINANCE NO. XXII.

RELATIVE TO THE GREEN BAY, MILWAUKEE AND CHICAGO RAILROAD.

Permission to locate road through city. SECTION 1. *Be it ordained by the common council of the city of Kenosha:* That the Green Bay, Milwaukee, and Chicago railroad company, be and are hereby permitted, as far as this city has the power to grant said permission, to locate their road through this city upon some one of the public streets on the following conditions, viz:

Not to alter grade of streets. That said company adopt as far as possible the same grade with their road as that of the street they may locate upon.

Not to put up buildings on streets. That they shall not erect any buildings or structures upon said street except the usual track of a railroad.

Not to obstruct ordinary use of street and to keep same in repair. That they shall locate, use, and occupy said railroad track so as not to interfere with the ordinary uses of said streets, and of the several cross streets, and shall keep the street so used in good and perfect repair as a street, so as to be used without inconvenience by citizens with all ordinary vehicles.

To build certain depots, store houses, &c. That said company shall erect as good, commodious and valuable buildings for depots, warehouses, and other buildings appurtenant to the railroad, as shall be erected by said company at any other place beside Milwaukee, and shall locate said depot and other buildings at some point within this city and south of Pine street; and shall generally afford the same accommodations with regard to the stoppage of all trains, and all other things as shall be offered to any other town or city, except Milwaukee.

When shall be required to make drawbridge.

Sec. 2. That in case said railroad company should construct said road across any part of the harbor or meandered portion of Pike Creek, that said company be required to construct and keep in repair a good and sufficient draw bridge, and have the same properly attended, so as at all times to allow the passage and re-passage of all vessels navigating said harbor.

In what case ordinance to be void.

Sec. 3. That this ordinance shall be void unless accepted by said company, and notice thereof in writing served upon the mayor of this city within thirty days from the date of its passage.

C. C. SHOLES, *Mayor.*

Passed August 1, 1853.

J. MURRAY, City Clerk.

ORDINANCE NO. XXIII.

RELATIVE TO REMOVING SNOW FROM SIDE-WALKS.

Owners or occupants of lots to remove snow.

SECTION 1. *Be it ordained by the common council of the city of Kenosha:* That it shall be the duty of owners or occupants of lots fronting on the streets set forth in the third section of this ordinance, to keep the side-walks in front of the lots clear of snow; and in case the side-walks against said lots shall at any time become obstructed with snow falling or drifting thereon, the owners or occupants of the lots shall cause the same to be cleaned within twenty-four hours thereafter.

When street supervisor shall remove snow.

Sec. 2. In case of the neglect of such owners or occupants of such lots to remove the obstruction set forth in the first section of this ordinance agreeably to the requisition of section first, it shall be the duty of the street supervisor of any ward where such obstruction may be found to cause the same to be removed as soon as may be reasonably done, and under oath shall make return to the clerk of the city of the expense of such removal, and the same shall be collected as other city taxes.

Expense, how collected.

Territory subject to ordinance.

Sec. 3. The side-walks and streets adjoining and fronting upon the following streets shall be subject to the provisions of this ordinance, to wit:

Market street, from the lake shore to West Main street.

Main street, from Lemon street, in the Second Ward, to the intersection of Main and Park avenue.

Park avenue, from the north side of block fifty-nine (59) in the third ward, to lot 36 on the north-east quarter of section 6, by Brande's map, in said Third Ward.

Wisconsin street, from Main street to the west side of block thirty-eight (38) on south-east quarter section thirty-one (31).

Park street, from the lake shore to West Main street.

West Main street, from Market street to Grand street.

Exchange street, from Market street to Deming street.

Ann street, from Prairie avenue to Grand street.

Grand street, from Main street to West Main street.

Chicago street, from Pearl street to Prairie avenue.

North end of the Park in the Third Ward, of said city, from Kenosha street to Chicago street.

Prairie avenue, from the west side of the Park in the Third Ward, to the west limits of the city.

Deming street, from Mechanic street to Park avenue.

Church street, from the Park to Market street.

GEO. H. PAUL, *Mayor.*

Passed March 20, 1858.

H. T. West, *City Clerk.*

ORDINANCE NO. XXIV.

AN ORDINANCE RELATING TO SIDE-WALKS.

When duty of council to levy a tax.

Section 1. *Be it ordained by the common council of the city of Kenosha:* Whenever any street supervisor of this city shall have made return to the clerk of the expenses of laying any side-walk, it shall be the duty of the clerk to lay such return before the common council, and the council shall thereupon proceed to levy a tax for the expense of such improvement, as provided in the city charter.

Duty of street supervisor when side-walks are out of repair.

Sec. 2. Whenever any side-walk in said city shall become broken or out of repair, it shall be the duty of the street supervisor of the ward in which such side-walk is located, to serve a notice upon the owner, occupant or agent of the lot or lots in front of which or part of which said side-walk runs, if they can be found in the city, directing him to repair such side-walk within forty-eight hours from the time of serving such notice; and if any such owner or occupant, as aforesaid, shall fail to comply with the direction of said supervisor to repair such side-walk, said owner or occupant shall be fined in the sum of five dollars; and it shall be the duty of the said supervisor, upon the failure of any such owner or occupant to repair such side-walk, to proceed forthwith and

and repair the same, and keep an accurate account of the expense of such repair in front of each lot, and shall make return to the common council of such expense, verified by his affidavit; and the said common council shall direct said expense to be levied and collected on such lots in the same manner as is provided in the city charter for levying and collecting expenses for building side-walks.

Sec. 3. Every street in this city of four rods in width, which shall hereafter be graded and improved shall be graded so as to have a space on each side thereof twelve feet for side-walks. Every street of three rods in width shall be graded so as to have a space on each side thereof eight feet in width for side-walks. **Width of side-walks established.**

GEO. H. PAUL, *Mayor.*

Passed March 20, 1858.

H. T. WEST, *City Clerk.*

ORDINANCE NO. XXV.

RELATIVE TO THE LEASING OF LAKE STREET DOCK.

SECTION 1. *Be it ordained by the common council of the city of Kenosha:* The agreement this day made between the harbor committee, on the part of the city and Wm. B. Slocum, for the lease to said **Confirmation of lease.**

Slocum of the north ninety (90) feet of Lake street in this city, which lease is signed by the harbor committee, and the seal of the city thereunto attached, is hereby fully confirmed in all its particulars by the common council.

V. HUGHES, *Mayor.*

Passed August 4, 1856.

H. T. WEST, *City Clerk.*

ORDINANCE NO. XXVI.

IN RELATION TO DOCKING.

Who may construct dock adjoining lot 3, block 9.

SECTION 1. *Be it ordained by the common council of the city of Kenosha:* That the proprietor or proprietors of lot three (3) in block nine (9) in the south-east quarter of section thirty-one (31) in the first ward of the city, be and hereby are authorized to construct a dock as follows: Commencing at a point twenty (20) feet west of the south-east corner of said block nine (9,) and extending thence northerly, parallel with the meandered line of the creek, to the north line of said block.

May also dock end of alley.

SEC. 2. Also, that the proprietors of lot three (3) in block nine (9) be and are hereby authorized to construct a dock across the west end of the alley, extending from east to west along the south side of said block nine (9,)and the exclusive use for docking purposes is hereby granted to said proprietors, which it is, however, understood shall not interfere with the free use of said alley for other purposes by the public.

Sec. 3. It is hereby provided, however, that the city does not by the passage of this ordinance agree to protect the owners of said lot in any rights or privileges herein granted against the legal claims of any person whatever. **Proviso.**

Sec. 4. It is hereby also provided that if the said docking be not completed within one year from the passage of this ordinance the same shall be null and void. **Limit of ordinance.**

V. HUGHES, *Mayor*,

Passed October 6, 1856.

H. T. West, City Clerk.

ORDINANCE NO. XXXII.

IN RELATION TO A TAX IN AID OF THE KENOSHA AND BELOIT RAILROAD.

Section 1, *Be it ordained by the common council of the city of Kenosha:* That under and in accordance with section 8 of "An act to amend the charter of the city of Kenosha," approved March 23, 1853, and section 44 of the "Act to incorporate the city of **$150,000 railroad tax levied.**

Kenosha," a question shall be submitted to the legal voters whether a tax to the amount of one hundred and fifty thousand dollars shall be levied and collected for the promotion of the common interest of the city in aid of the Kenosha and Beloit railroad, as follow, viz: fifty thousand dollars in 1856, fifty thousand dollars in 1857, and fifty thousand dollars in 1858.

Question to be submitted.

Sec. 2. The election for this purpose shall be held on Tuesday the 28th day of August, instant, in the 1st ward at the City Hall, in the 2d ward, basement of Mr. N. R. Allen's dwelling house, and in the 3d ward at No. 2. Engine house. The polls shall be opened at 9 A. M. of said day and closed at 12 M., opened again at 1 P. M. and finally closed at 5 P. M, The qualifications of voters are as prescribed by section 44 of the act last above referred to, and the election shall be conducted generally as other elections in said city are conducted for city purposes. The ballots shall have written or printed thereon the words "For tax as provided by ordinance," or "Against tax."

If approved mayor to take stock for city.

Sec. 3. Upon the return and canvass of the votes cast, if it shall appear that a majority of the legal votes have voted for such tax, the mayor shall, in the name of the city of Kenosha, subscribe to the capital stock of the Kenosha and Beloit railroad company, the sum of sixty-six thousand dollars, for which stock, on the reception by the treasurer of this city, full paid certificates covering said sum, the mayor and clerk shall issue and deliver to the railroad company city scrip in such denominations as the proper officers of said company may request, as follows:— Twenty-two thousand dollars payable first of January A. D. 1857; twenty-two thousand dollars payable first of January A. D. 1858; and twenty-two thousand dollars payable first day of January, A. D. 1859; said scrip to bear an interest of 10 per cent., and the interest to be paid annually.

Shall issue scrip therefor.

Sec. 4. The mayor shall further subscribe to the stock of said company, in the name of the city, the sum of eighty-four thousand dollars, said amount being understood to cover the stock subscriptions for which freeholders of this city are now responsible, and have in part paid; but it is hereby expressly provided that the city is to pay of such subscriptions only such part as may remain unpaid, and as shall be collected from year to year under the provisions of section 1 of this ordinance, in the shape of tax, and to such amount, in each individual case, as shall have been collected from the real estate property of such freeholder or tax payer; said city, at the time or times of such payment, to receive in its own name from some railroad company certificates of stock for the amount of money so paid.

Further subscription by mayor.

Proviso.

Sec. 5. In collecting the taxes provided for by the first section of this ordinance, the city treasurer shall receive as cash, at par value, with interest, any of the scrip of the proper year, hereinbefore provided to be issued; and also, at their face, on, or in full of such

In what, and how tax may be paid

tax, receipts of the treasurer of said railroad company, specifying the sum with interest which such person, who offers said receipt, shall have paid on his subscription to the stock, as, at the date of this ordinance, appears in his name on the stock subscription book or books of the railroad company.

When payor entitled to stock certificate.

Sec. 6. Upon the payment of tax in cash, or city railroad scrip of the proper year as above provided, by any freeholder or real estate tax payer of this city, of an amount sufficient to cover the face and interest of a certificate or certificates of stock in the hands of the city treasurer, said freeholder or freeholders, or real estate tax payer shall be entitled to receive, and may demand from said treasurer, any such certificate or certificates, and the city treasurer is hereby authorized to make the necessary transfer thereof. On the final settlement of the tax account under this ordinance, the stock certificates remaining in the city treasury shall then be divided among the freeholders or real estate tax payers, in such manner and proportion as shall be just and equitable, according to the amount of assessment upon the real estate of each, and the tax collected or realized therefrom. Until such division or distribution shall have been made, the certificates of stock in the hands of the city shall be voted upon at all meetings of stockholders as the mayor and council shall determine and direct.

Council may direct how stock shall be represented.

Compensation of treasurer.

Sec. 7. For the performance of all duties under this ordinance, the city treasurer shall not receive to exceed two hundred and fifty dollars per annum.

C. C. SHOLES, *Mayor.*

Passed August 16, 1855.

J. MURRAY, City Clerk.

ORDINANCE NO. *XXXIV.*

AUTHORIZING THE ISSUE OF CITY BONDS FOR HARBOR PURPOSES.

(1857.) Issue of $10,000 bonds for harbor purposes authorized.

Section 1. *Be it ordained by the Common Council of the city of Kenosha :* For the purpose of the further improvement of the harbor at the mouth of Pike creek in this city, and for other expenses connected therewith, the common council is hereby authorized to issue city bonds, to an amount not exceeding the sum of ten thousand dollars, and to pledge the resources and credit of the city for the payment thereof, with interest as hereinafter provided.

How to be executed and issued.

Sec. 2. Every bond issued under the authority contained in the preceding section shall be made payable in ten years from the date thereof, with interest payable annually, at the rate of ten per cent. per annum, at such place or places as the council shall direct, and shall be signed by the mayor and countersigned by the clerk, under the corporate seal of the city.

Question to be submitted to the people.

Sec. 3. The foregoing sections of this ordinance shall not be in force until the question of the issue f such bonds shall be submitted to such voters of the city of Kenosha as are possessed of a freehold estate, or occupy lots upon leases on which lots they pay taxes—as provided by section 44 of the city charter, and by the act of March 23, 1853, amendatory thereof—at an election to be held for that purpose, at a time hereinafter provided; and adopted by a majority of the votes cast at such election.

Election, when and how to be held.

Sec. 4. An election shall be held on Tuesday the 10th day of February proximo, between the hours of ten A. M. and four o'clock in the afternoon of said day, at the places in the several wards of the city where the last elections were held, for the purpose of determining whether such bonds shall be issued as provided by the first two sections of this ordinance, and such election shall be conducted, and the votes canvassed and returned in the same manner and by the same officers, as at other elections.

Form of ballot.

Sec. 5. On the ballots which shall be received by the inspectors of such election shall be either written or printed, the words, "For the issue of bonds," or the words, "Against the issue of bonds."

When ordinance to be of force.

Sec. 6. At the next meeting of the common council after the returns of such election have been made, the common council shall proceed to canvass such return, and if it is found that a majority of the whole of the vote taken are "For the issue of bonds," this ordinance shall be in force from and after such canvass.

V. HUGHES, Mayor.

Passed January 24, 1857.

H. T. WEST, City Clerk.

ORDINANCE NO. XXXV.

RELATING TO THE BONDS ISSUED IN AID OF THE KENOSHA AND BELOIT RAILROAD COMPANY.

SECTION 1. *Be it ordained by the common council of the city of Kenosha:* That the change of name of the Kenosha and Beloit railroad company to the Kenosha and Rockford railroad company, and the change of destination of the said road from Beloit to Rockford, and the consolidation of the said Kenosha and Rockford railroad company with the Kenosha and Rockford railroad company of Illinois, be each andall of them severally and collectively approved and ratifiedby this council. Change of name of company approved.

SEC. 2. That the said Kenosha and Rockford rail road company, or the Kenosha, Rockford and Rock Island railroad company, as successors of the said Kenosha and Beloit railroad company, be, and they are hereby fully authorized and empowered to use, sell or otherwise dispose of the city bonds, issued in aid of the Kenosha and Beloit railroad company as fully and entirely as the said Kenosha and Beloit railroad might or could do. New company may use bonds as did the old.

SEC. 3. This ordinance shall be submitted to the qualified electors of this city at the election to be held on Tuesday next, for their approval. Question to be submitted.

SEC 4. Such election, so far as it relates to this ordinance, shall be conducted, and the returns there- Manner and form of election and ballot.

of made in the same manner as other elections held under the city charter; and on the ballots relating to this ordinance shall either be written or printed, "For the railroad ordinance," or, "Against the railroad ordinance."

When ordinance to be of force, &c. Sec. 5. If a majority of such ballots cast are "For the railroad ordinance," this ordinance shall be in force from and after the time the council shall have canvassed the returns of such election.

SHELDON FISH, *Acting Mayor.*

Passed April 1, 1857.

H. T. WEST, *City Clerk.*

ORDINANCE NO. XXXVII.

AUTHORIZING THE ISSUE OF CITY BONDS IN AID OF THE KENOSHA AND ROCKFORD RAIL ROAD.

[1857.] Issue of city bonds to amount of $100,000 authorized. SECTION 1, *Be it ordained by the common council of the city of Kenosha:* That the mayor and clerk are hereby authorized to issue city bonds to the amount of one hundred thousand dollars, and to pledge the resources and credit of the city for the payment thereof with interest, as hereinafter provided.

Bonds, when payable, &c. Sec. 2. Every bond issued under the authority contained in the preceding section shall be made payable in twenty years from the date thereof, with interest at the rate of seven per cent. per annum payable semi-annually at such place or places as the common council shall direct, and shall be signed by the mayor and countersigned by the clerk under the corporate seal of the city

Sec. 3. An amount of said bonds equal to the amount of railroad scrip issued in 1856, now outstanding and unpaid, shall be delivered to the Kenosha and Rockford railroad company as soon as said company shall deliver up the full amount of said scrip to the city of Kenosha, or furnish to the council satisfactory security for the cancellation of the same with the interest thereon: and thereafter the remainder of such bonds issued as hereinbefore provided shall be delivered to said Kenosha and Rockford railroad company as soon as said company shall execute to the city of Kenosha a bond and a mortgage for an amount of not more than ten thousand dollars per mile upon such portion of said road in the state of Wisconsin as the council shall select as security for the payment of principal and interest of said last named amount of bonds, said mortgage to be second only to a prior mortgage of ten thousand dollars per mile, and to cover the rolling stock, depot grounds, and all other appurtenances belonging to said road.

Bonds, when and on what conditions may be delivered to railroad Co.

Sec. 4. All that part of an ordinance passed August 16, 1855, entitled "An ordinance in relation to a tax in aid of the Kenosha and Beloit railroad," which relates to the levy and collection of a tax in the years 1857 and 1858 for the promotion of the

Repeal in part of ordinance levying railroad tax for 1857 and 1858.

common interest of the city in aid of the Kenosha and Beloit railroad, is hereby repealed.

Ordinance of force, only on submission to a vote of approval.

Sec. 5. The foregoing sections of this ordinance shall not be in force until the question of the issue of such bonds shall be submitted to such voters of the city of Kenosha as are possessed of a freehold estate, or occupy lots upon leases, upon which lots they pay taxes, as provided by the present city charter, at an election to be held for that purpose at a time hereinafter provided, and adopted by a majority of the votes cast at such election.

Elections when and how held.

Sec. 6. An election shall be held on Thursday, the 2d day of July, 1857, between the hours of one and six o'clock in the afternoon of said day, at the places in the several wards of the city where the last election was held, for the purpose of determining whether such bonds shall be issued as provided by this ordinance, and such election shall be conducted and the votes canvassed and returned in the same manner and by the same officers as at other elections.

Form of ballots.

Sec. 7. On the ballots which shall be received by the inspectors of such election shall be either written or printed the words "For the issue of bonds," or the words "Against the issue of bonds."

Validity of ordinance, how ascertained.

Sec. 8. At the next meeting of the common council after the returns of such election shall have been made, the common council shall proceed to canvass such returns, and if it is found that a majority of the whole of the votes take taken are for the issue of bonds, this ordinance shall be in force from and after such canvass.

GEO. H. PAUL, *Mayor.*

Passed June 23, 1857.

H. T. WEST, *City Clerk.*

ORDINANCE NO. XXXVIII.

TO AMEND AN ORDINANCE AUTHORIZING THE ISSUE OF CITY BONDS IN AID OF THE KENOSHA & ROCKFORD RAILROAD, PASSED JUNE 23, 1857.

Rate of interest on $100,000 bonds changed.

SECTION 1. *Be it ordained by the common council of the city of Kenosha:* Section second of an ordinance entitled, "An ordinance authorizing the issue of city bonds in aid of the Kenosha and Rockford railroad," passed June 23, 1857, is hereby amended by striking out the word "seven," and inserting "ten," so as to make the bonds issued under said ordinance draw ten per cent. interest, payable semi-annually, instead of seven per cent.

Amendment to section 3 of ordinance referred to.

SEC. 2. Section third of said ordinance, passed June 23, 1857, is hereby amended by striking out the words, "the amount of railroad scrip issued in 1856, now outstanding and unpaid," and inserting in lieu thereof, the words "thirty-five thousand dollars," also by striking out the words, "said scrip," and inserting in lieu thereof, the words, "the railroad scrip now outstanding and unpaid."

Question of amendment to be submitted.

Sec. 3. The foregoing sections of this ordinance shall not be in force until the question of the amendments therein provided for shall be submitted to such voters of the city of Kenosha as are possessed of a freehold estate, or occupy lots upon leases on which lots they pay taxes, as provided by the city charter, at an election to be held for that purpose at a time hereinafter provided, and adopted by a majority of the votes cast at such election.

Election, when and how held.

Sec. 4. An election shall be held on the 17th day of August inst., between the hours of one and six o'clock in the afternoon of said day, at the places in the several wards of the city where the last elections were held, for the purpose of determining the question of such amendments, and such election shall be conducted and the votes canvassed and returned in the same manner and by the same officers as at other elections.

Form of ballots.

Sec. 5. On the ballots which shall be received by the inspectors of such election, shall be either written or printed, the words, "For the amendments to railroad ordinance," or "Against the amendments to railroad ordinance."

When amendments to be of force.

Sec. 6. At the next meeting of the common council after the returns of such election have been made, the common council shall proceed to canvass such return, and if it is found that a majority of all the votes taken are for the amendments to railroad ordinance, this ordinance shall be in force from and after such canvass.

GEO. H. PAUL, *Mayor.*

Passed August 13, 1857.

H. T. WEST, *City Clerk.*

ORDINANCE NO. XXXIX.

AMENDING THE ORDINANCE IN RELATION TO STREET SUPERVISORS AND THEIR DUTIES.

Section 1. *Be it ordained by the common council of the city of Kenosha:* That the ordinance entitled "An ordinance relating to street supervisors and their duties" is hereby amended so as to provide that any person in default of the payment of any judgment or fine against him for the non-payment of poll tax, may be imprisoned for a term of not less than two days nor exceeding ten days, at the discretion of the justice.

Persons refusing to pay poll tax may be imprisoned.

Sect 2. The substance of the amendment to said ordinance contained in the previous section shall, in the book of revised ordinances now being published, be incorporated in the ordinance to which this ordi-

Amendment to be published in revised ordinances.

nance is amendatory, as a part of the original ordinance.

GEO. H. PAUL, *Mayor.*

Passed June 21, 1858.

C. B. LEWIS, *City Clerk.*

ORDINANCE NO. XLII.

AN ORDINANCE TO AMEND ORDINANCE NO. 19, TO REGULATE AND RESTRAIN RUNNERS OR SOLICITORS.

Runers not to interfere with persons or baggage.

SECTION 1. *Be it ordained by the common council of the city of Kenosha:* Ordinance No. 19 of the revised series is hereby amended by the addition of Sec. 4, as follows: Every person who shall be engaged in the business of runner or solicitor who shall in any manner interfere or meddle with any person or persons on the railroad cars or steamboats, or with their baggage until such baggage is set apart to the owner thereof by the proper person having charge of the same, or who shall go on said cars or steamboats with the intention of soliciting any person or persons to go to any hotel or other place, or who shall go within the bounds or limits designated by the person or persons having control of said railroad depot or station or steamboat landing, for the purpose of so running or soliciting, shall on conviction pay a fine not exceeding ten dollars nor less than three dollars to be recovered as provided by chapter 13 of the city charter, and the common council may from time to time appoint one or more special policemen more effectually to carry out the provisions of the ordinance to which this is amendatory: *Provided,* That nothing shall be paid to such policemen as compensation in cases arising under this ordinance, except where an actual arrest is made for a breach of any of its provisions. Fine for violation of ordinance.

GEO. H. PAUL, *Mayor.*

Passed September 20, 1858.

C. B. LEWIS, *City Clerk.*

ORDINANCE NO. XLIV.

RELATING TO LICENSING AND TAXING AUCTIONEERS.

Section 1. *Be it ordained by the common council of the city of Kenosha:* There shall be paid into the city treasury, for the use of the city of Kenosha, upon all sales by auction of goods, wares, or merchandise, three per cent. of the moneys arising rom said sales out of said moneys: Provided, that License to be paid for selling at auction.

nothing herein shall extend to any sale by auction of goods, wares, or merchandise, made by virtue of any rule, order, decree or judgment of any court, or made by virtue of any law, respecting the collection of taxes, or to any sale by auction of property belonging to the United States, or this State, or made by or in behalf of any executor or administrator, or made in consequence of any general assignment of property or effects for the benefit of creditors: *Provided*, The goods, wares and merchandise assigned were in the county of Kenosha at the time of such assignment.

Auctioneer must have license. Sec. 2. No person shall hereafter act as auctioneer, or sell or exhibit for sale, at public auction or vendue, within the city of Kenosha, any goods, wares or merchandise, unless such person shall have license therefor from the mayor. Any person violating the provisions of this section, shall forfeit and pay to the city, for each and every offence, and for each and every day he may act as auctioneer or exhibit and sell at public auction or vendue, any goods, wares or merchandize the sum of thirty dollars, besides costs of suit in addition to the tax imposed by this ordinance: *Provided*, That no license shall be required for sales at auction of any goods, wares or merchandize which by this ordinance are not made liable to tax or duty.

Mayor may license auctioneer. Sec. 3. The mayor is authorized to license any person residing in the city to act as auctioneer:—*Provided*, That the person desiring to be licensed shall first pay the sum of five dollars and execute to the city of Kenosha a bond in the penal sum of five hundred dollars, with two securities to be approved by the common council, conditioned, that the person so licensed shall pay the tax or duty imposed by this ordinance, and comply with the provisions of the same.

Sec. 4. Every person so licensed, shall monthly on the first Monday of each month, render under oath to the city treasurer, a true and full account of all goods, wares or merchandize liable to pay duties by this ordinance, sold by him during the preceding month, or subsequent to the last monthly statement, and shall at the same time pay over to the city treasurer the amount of such duty or tax.

Auctioneer must render report of sales.

Sec. 5. It shall be the duty of the city treasurer on the first Monday in each month, to demand from each auctioneer or person employed in the auction business, the statement and the tax or duty specified in the foregoing section, and shall enter the amount of the tax or duty so received to the credit of the general fund of the city.

Duty of Treasurer in relation to auctioneers.

Sec. 6. No license shall be granted for a less term than one year.

License must be for one year.

Sec. 7. In all cases where the auctioneer or owner of the property sold, or any person employed by them or either of them, shall become the purchaser of the property sold at such sale, it shall be subject to the same tax or duty as if any other person had become the purchaser.

Owner or auctioneer when purchasers must pay duty.

Sec. 8. The sale book of any auctioneer shall be

Sale book of auctioneer must kept open for inspection.

open to the inspection of the city treasurer, and in case the treasurer shall have reason to believe that the monthly statement of the auctioneer is untrue or incorrect, he shall charge such auctioneer such sum as he may deem just and proper according to the provisions of this ordinance.

GEO. H. PAUL, *Mayor.*

Passed February 21, 1859.

C. B. LEWIS, City Clerk.

ORDINANCE NO. XLVII.

VACATING A PORTION OF LAKE STREET IN THE FIRST WARD OF THE CITY OF KENOSHA.

Section 1. *Be it ordained by the common council of the city of Kenosha:* That all that portion of Lake street, between Park street and Wisconsin street, and lying east of block No. (10) ten, in the south-west quarter of section No. (32) thirty-two town (2) two, range (23) twenty-three, in the first ward of the city of Kenosha, be and is hereby declared vacated.

A. FARR, Mayor.

Passed May 16, 1859.

C. B. LEWIS, City Clerk.

ORDINANCE NO. LIV.

PRESCRIBING THE FIRE LIMITS OF THE CITY OF KENOSHA.

Fire limits defined.

Section 1. *Be it ordained by the common council of the city of Kenosha :* That all that part of the city embraced in the following limits, shall hereafter be known as the fire limits in said city, to wit:—Commencing at a point where the centre of Main and Grand streets meet, thence along the centre of Main street to the Kenosha, Rockford and Rock Island railroad, thence east 165 feet, thence south parallel with the centre of said Main street to South street, thence west along the centre of said South street to a point 165 feet west of the centre of Main street, thence north to Grand street parallel to said centre of Main street, thence east along said centre of Grand street to place of beginning; also the south half of blocks 26 and 27 fronting on Market or Exchange streets, and the north half of blocks 30 and 31 fronting on Market street and Market square, not included in the limits just described.

New building in fire limits must be built of brick or stone.

Sec. 2. All buildings which shall hereafter be erected, placed or put upon any lot or lots within the above defined fire limits, shall, except by special vote of the council be constructed with walls of brick or stone, or other incombustible material, and no wooden building now standing within said limits shall be removed from the place where it now is unless removed without said fire limits; nor shall any such building be removed into the fire limits, nor shall any building within said limits be enlarged with wooden materials.

Wood or lumber not to be piled on vacant lots in fire limits.

Sec. 3. No person shall place or put upon any vacant lot or lots or parts of lots within the foregoing prescribed fire limits, any wood, lumber or other combustible material except such as are necessary for immediate use.

Sheds or privies may be built in fire limits.

Sec. 4. Sheds not exceeding twelve feet in height at the peak or highest part thereof, and privies not exceeding ten feet square and twelve feet in height at the peak, may be constructed of wood, and shall not be subject to the provisions of this ordinance:—*Provided,* That the term shed be so construed as to mean a structure with a roof sloping one way, with one or more sides of the said structure entirely open. But all depositories for ashes within said fire limits shall be built of brick or other fire proof material.

Penalty.

Sec. 5. Any person who shall violate any of the provisions of this ordinance shall pay a fine of not less than ten or more than one hundred dollars, and in default of the payment thereof shall be imprisoned not more than thirty nor less than five days, or until such fine and all costs are paid.

Sec. 6. Any wooden building which may be erected, enlarged or renovated or in process of erection, enlargment or removal, contrary to this ordinance, or any wood, lumber or other combustible material placed or put upon any vacant lot or lots contrary to this ordinance shall be deemed a nuisance, and upon information it shall be the duty of the mayor after due notice to the owner or builder thereof to abate the same by an order in writing to require the city marshal to raze such building to the ground, and to remove the wood, lumber or other combustibles from the vacant lot or lots within the said fire limits. The expense of such removal in either case shall be reported by the marshal for assessment and may be collected of the owner of such building lot or lots by suit.

Duty of Mayor in premises.

Sec. 7. All ordinances heretofore passed conflicting herewith shall be and the same are hereby repealed.

I. W. WEBSTER, Mayor.

Passed February 18, 1861.

C. B. Lewis, City Clerk.

ORDINANCE NO. LVIII.

FOR PAYING BOUNTIES TO VOLUNTEERS.

City scrip to be issued to pay bounties to volunteers.

Section 1. *Be it ordained by the common council of the city of Kenosha :* Fro the purpose of paying a bounty of $200 to each of such volunteers as may have been mustered into the military service of the United States since October 17th, 1863, or that shall hereafter be mustered into said service, who may have been or shall hereafter be credited to said city, upon her quota of volunteers to be raised since said 17th day of October, 1863, the common council is hereby authorized and empowered to issue city scrip to an amount not exceeding $10,000, and to negotiate the same upon reasonable terms, and levy and collect a tax upon the last assessment of said city, upon all the taxable property thereof, in the same manner as other taxes are levied and collected, for the purpose of paying said scrip so to be issued as aforesaid, or such bounty of $200 to any one volunteer.

Question of issuing scrip to be submitted to voters.

Sec. 2. The foregoing section of this ordinance shall not be in force until the question of the issuing of such scrip or levying and collecting such tax shall be submitted to the legal voters of said city of Kenosha, as provided by law, at an election to be held for that purpose, at a time hereinafter provided, and adopted by a majority of the votes cast at such election.

Sec. 3. An election shall be held on the 26th day of February, 1864, between the hours of nine o'clock A. M., and four o'clock P. M., in the several wards of the city at the following places: Where election shall be held.

1st Ward, at the Council Room;

2nd Ward, at C. Schend's;

3rd Ward, at office of H. Durkee in said ward;

4th Ward, at N. R. Allen's;

for the purpose of determining whether such scrip shall be issued and tax levied and collected, as provided by the first two sections of this ordinance, and such election shall be conducted in the same manner as other elections.

Sec. 4. On the ballots which shall be received by the inspectors, shall be written or printed the words "For Bounty Ordinance," or "Against Bounty Ordinance." Ballots.

Sec. 5. At the next meeting, special or general, of the common council, after the returns of such election have been made, the common council shall proceed to canvass such returns, and if it is found that a majority of the whole vote taken is for the Bounty Ordinance, this ordinance shall be in force from and after such canvass. When council to canvass votes.

F. ROBINSON, Mayor.

Passed February 19, 1864.

C. B. LEWIS, City Clerk.

57

ORDERS

OF THE

COMMON COUNCIL.

ORDERS OF THE COMMON COUNCIL.

ORDER NO. I.

It is hereby ordered by the common council of the city of Kenosha: That a street be opened, the centre of which shall commence at a point four hundred and eighty (480) feet south of the north-west corner of the south-west quarter of the north-east quarter of section six (6), township one (1), range twenty-three (23), on the west line of the city of Kenosha,—thence east to Kenosha street, to a point seventy-seven feet south of the south-east corner of land sold by J. P. Bishop to H. K. Torrey—said street to be four rods wide.

V. HUGHES, *Mayor*,

Passed May 5, 1856.

H. T. WEST, City Clerk.

ORDER NO. II.

It is hereby ordered by the common council of the city of Kenosha: That a street be opened on the west side of the ground taken as the depot for the Green Bay, Milwaukee & Chicago railroad, on the south-west quarter of section thirty-one (31)—said street commencing on the north line of said south-west quarter, in the centre of Grand street, at a point sixteen (16) rods west of the north-east corner of said quarter, and extending southerly thirty-eight (38) rods—said street to be four rods wide.

V. HUGHES, *Mayor.*

Passed April 21, 1856.

H. T. West, *City Clerk.*

ORDER NO. III.

It is hereby ordered by the common council of the city of Kenosha: That a street be laid out, commencing thirty-eight (38) rods south of the north-east corner of the south-west quarter of section thirty-one (31), to be four rods in width, and extend to the west line of the corporation, said street to be called Garden street.

V. HUGHES, *Mayor.*

Passed April 21, 1856.

H. T. West, *City Clerk.*

ORDER NO. IV.

It is hereby ordered by the common council of the city of Kenosha: That an alley be laid out through block twenty-four (24), south-east quarter of section thirty-one (31) in the first ward of the city of Kenosha, said alley to be twelve feet in width, and to run east and west through the centre of said block.

V. HUGHES, *Mayor.*

Passed April 21, 1856.

H. T. West, *City Clerk.*

ORDER NO. V.

It is hereby ordered by the common council of the city of Kenosha: That a street be laid out from east to west through the centre of block thirty-one, in the south-east quarter of section thirty, township two north, of range twenty-three (23), in the second ward of the city of Kenosha. Said street to be three rods wide.

V. HUGHES, *Mayor.*

Passed May 13, 1856.

C. B. Lewis, *City Clerk.*

ORDER NO. VII.

It is hereby ordered by the common council of the city of Kenosha: That the alley between lots 5 and 6 in block 86, in the north east quarter of section 31, and in the 2d ward of the city of Kenosha, be, and the same is hereby vacated.

V. HUGHES, Mayor.

Passed June 16, 1856.

H. T. WEST, City Clerk.

ORDER NO. XII.

It is hereby ordered by the common council of the city of Kenosha: That the north half of that portion of the alley which bounds on the south lots Nos. 2 and 3, block 9, south-east quarter of section 31, be vacated. *Provided:* That the warehouse now in process of construction by Kimball & Quarles on said lots shall not extend northward as far by thirteen feet, as the most northern pile now driven on either of said lots; and that the dock to be constructed on said lots, by said Kimball & Quarles, shall not extend northerly beyond the said most northerly pile now driven.

GEO. H. PAUL, Mayor.

Passed May 25, 1857.

H. T. WEST, City Clerk.

ORDER NO. XIV.

It is hereby ordered by the common council of the city of Kenosha: That Elizabeth street, on Seminary addition, be extended east across West Main street, and across block five in Holmes and Nichols' addition to said city, to meet a street on said last named addition, running east and west, and that the whole be called Elizabeth street.

GEO. H. PAUL, Mayor.

Passed August 17, 1857.

H. T. WEST, City Clerk.

ORDER NO. XVII.

It is hereby ordered by the common council of the city of Kenosha: That an alley in block 48 in the third ward of said city, running east and west, be and the same is hereby vacated.

GEO. H. PAUL, Mayor.

Passed November 6, 1857.

H, T. WEST, City Clerk.

ADDENDUM.

After the word "Horse" in the third line of section 6, Ordinance No. 14, read the words "ox, steer, cow, heifer, or bull; and after the word "horse" in the fifth line of said section insert "ox, steer, cow, heifer, or bull.

ERRATUM.

For odinance following ordinance No. 6, read ordinance No. 7, instead of No. "2."

INDEX.

INDEX.

INDEX TO ORDERS.

www.ingramcontent.com/pod-product-compliance
Lightning Source LLC
LaVergne TN
LVHW010743120826
845150LV00009B/1681
* 9 7 8 1 4 2 5 5 1 3 5 2 8 *